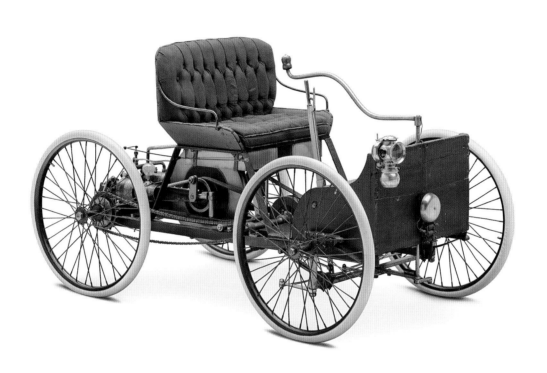

DRIVING AMERICA

THE HENRY FORD AUTOMOTIVE COLLECTION

CONTENTS

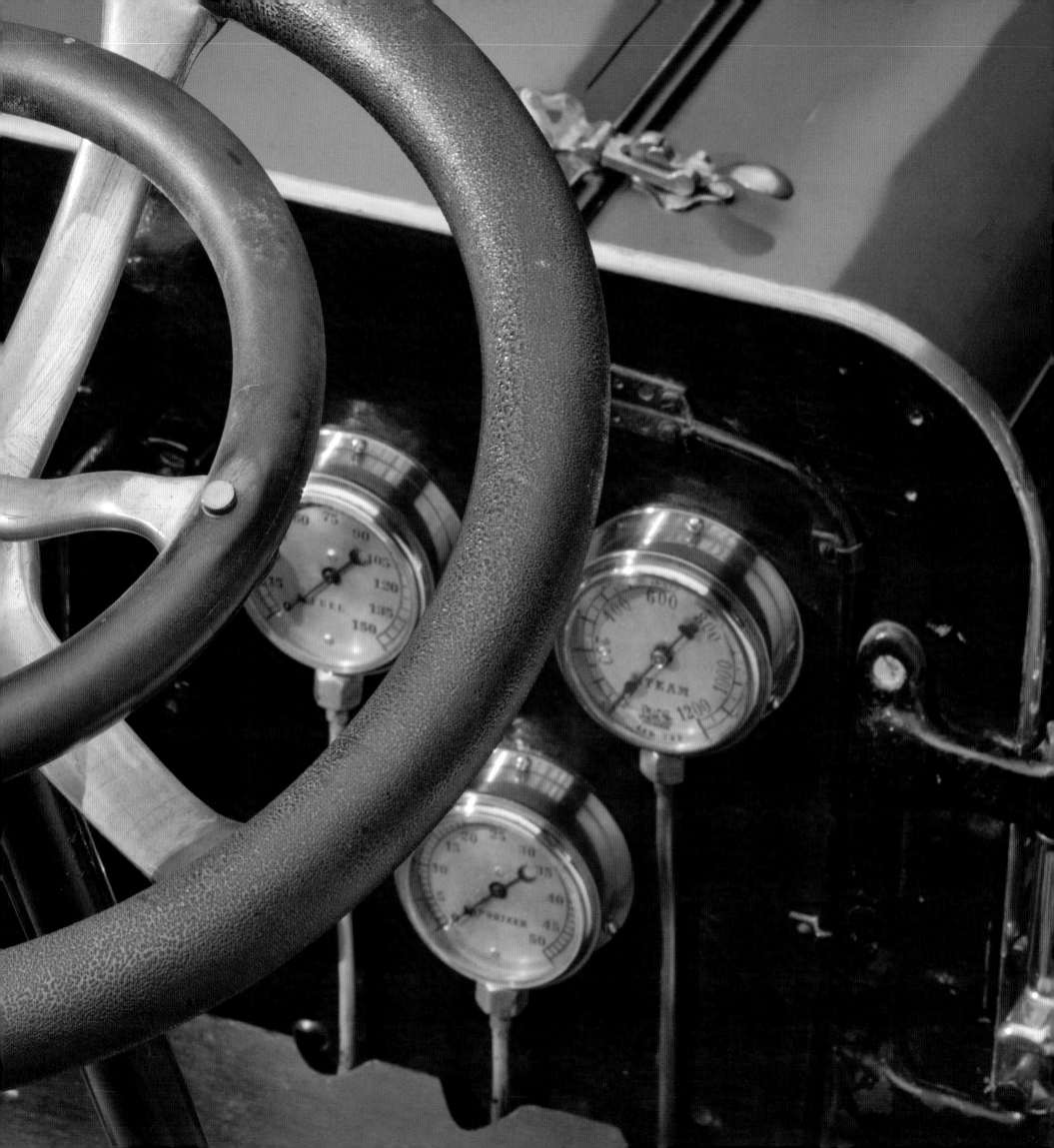

FOREWORD
BY JAY LENO

GROWING UP AS A KID IN A RURAL TOWN OUTSIDE OF ANDOVER, MASSACHUSETTS, I considered the automobile to be, quite simply, my freedom. When I needed to do something or be by myself, instead of just going up to my room or out to the backyard, I could get in my car and go to the next town. I could go to a friend's house. I could go to North Andover. I could go wherever I chose.

Most kids today dive into their iPhone or iPod when they want to escape. Us? We got into our car. For people of my generation, the car was our iPhone.

As a car enthusiast and a collector, I believe that The Henry Ford's automotive collection is one of the most important in the world. It is authentic. I can walk into Henry Ford Museum and see cars as they existed when they were created, with their mechanical assemblies and finishes perfectly preserved. The 1907 White Steamer, collected by Henry Ford himself, is just like the one I own—and I'm thrilled to be able to look at that car and know that it has been preserved 100 percent. I can see how it was put together when it was built. I can also see a Model T with every nut in place, exactly the way Henry Ford built it when it rolled off the assembly line. The Henry Ford preserves history 100 percent.

Maybe most important, the museum makes the story of the automobile fascinating—even to those who aren't fascinated by the automobile. Everyone can relate to something in the collection, because all the cars were selected for the amazing stories they represent.

What I personally love about The Henry Ford is that it's not a rich man's display filled with top-of-the-line automobiles. Instead, it's a collection of everyday stories, simple and extraordinary, that represent what makes this country great. There are fancy cars like the 1931 Bugatti Type 41 Royale, but there are also cars like the 1924 Essex Coach, which may seem insignificant until you realize that Essex was the first car company to make a closed car cheap and affordable—and this provided competition for the first time in the open ragtop car market.

From its steam engine collection that powered America's manufacturing to the actual bus on which Rosa Parks refused to give up her seat, The Henry Ford shows the whole story of America's growth, not just a chapter of it. This place reveals both the basic bread and butter of everyday life and the significant social and technological innovations that changed the very fabric of our nation. It takes us from experiencing the pure freedom we all felt in owning our first cars to the surprising realization that subcompacts like the 1978 Dodge Omni do indeed matter.

The Henry Ford is the story of us. It's the story of America.

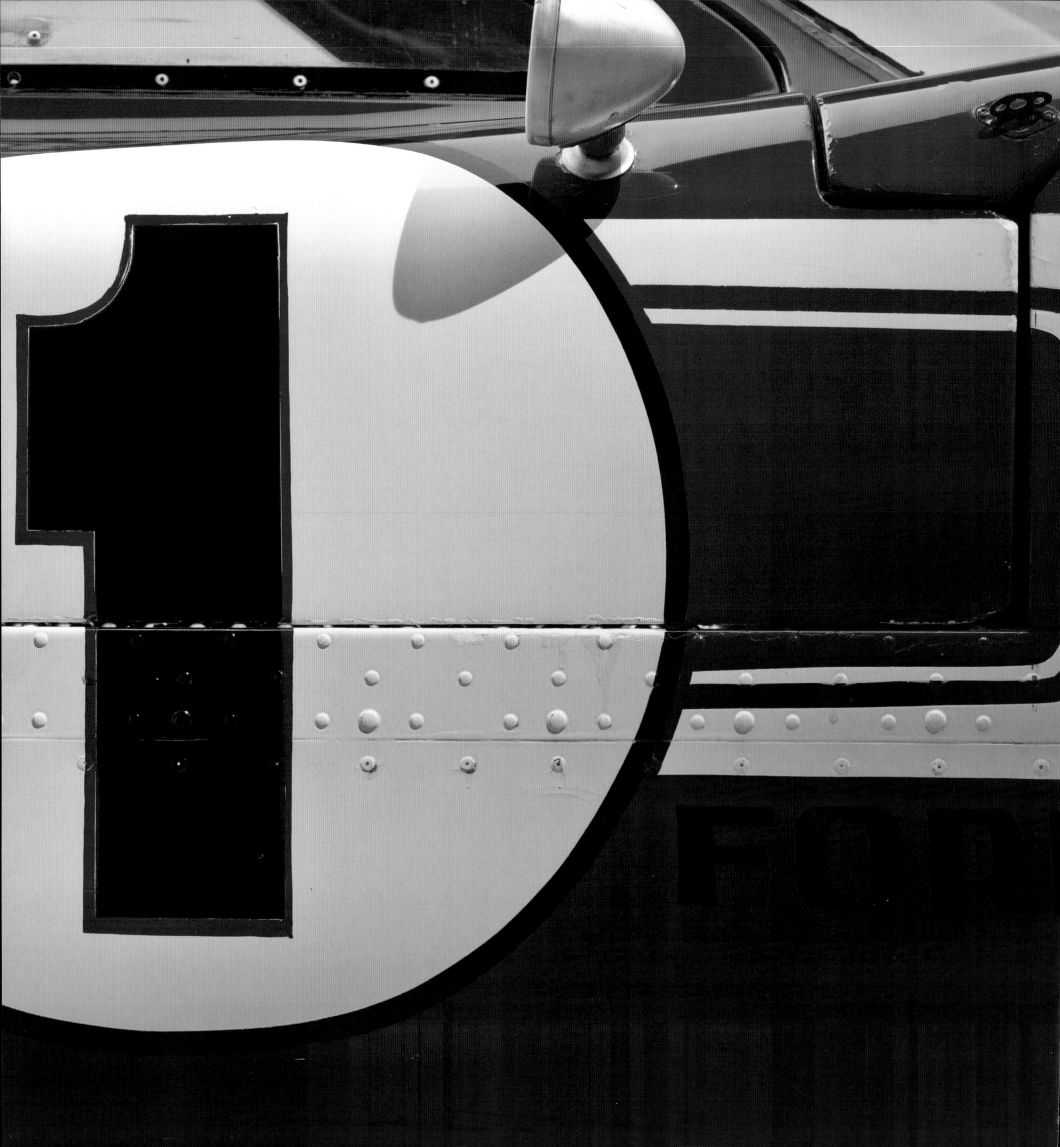

INTRODUCTION
By Edsel B. Ford II
Trustee of The Henry Ford

WHEN YOU GROW UP WITH A NAME LIKE MINE IN DETROIT, MICHIGAN, THERE IS AN ASSUMPTION you will end up involved in the automobile business. I feel fortunate that in my case, the assumption was true. I have spent my life in and around the automobile industry, and I continue to have a passion for it.

Automobiles are certainly the Ford family business. My great-grandfather, Henry Ford, pretty much determined that for all of us when he started the Ford Motor Company in 1903. Six generations later, we are still as passionate about our company as ever. Henry Ford was not just interested in building and selling automobiles. He was committed to what this new form of transportation could do for America and even the world. His vision of opening the highways to all humankind—using automobiles to allow ordinary families to travel great distances and see new things—changed this country forever.

In the generations since, the automobile has been revered and celebrated as part of our American culture in music and movies, with hot rods and custom cars, and in gatherings as simple as local car clubs and as grand as the fifty thousand vehicles that flock to the Woodward Dream Cruise in Detroit every year. The Henry Ford's automotive collection celebrates all those things, as well as the innovation and technology the industry has helped develop over the years, such as steam cars, internal combustion engines, hybrid power, and fully-electric and solar cars. We also celebrate the influence automobile racing has had in America, from the paradigm-setting cars of the early 1900s to the modern, three-hundred-plus mile-per-hour race cars of today.

The ingenuity, the passion, the people, and the companies who helped create the industry itself are celebrated here in the heart of the Motor City in a way no other place can do it. As a trustee of The Henry Ford, I am extremely proud of how this industry and the car culture itself—which is so important to our family—are portrayed and preserved, both in this book and in Henry Ford Museum's *Driving America* exhibition. I hope you enjoy our collection. And after you've experienced it in this book, please come and visit often.

An American Story

By Patricia E. Mooradian

President • The Henry Ford

I BOUGHT MY FIRST CAR THE DAY AFTER I GRADUATED FROM COLLEGE. It was a silver Mazda GLC. I felt so proud and free. This car was mine—not something I had to share with my four sisters, like the family station wagon we had growing up in Pennsylvania.

I don't really remember why I chose the Mazda for my first car. Whatever the reason, I'm sure it was the right car for the right price at the right time in my life.

I'm often reminded of my GLC as I stroll through The Henry Ford's *Driving America* exhibition. Located in Henry Ford Museum, it contains some of the vehicles you'll see on the following pages of this book. This exhibition is a story of us—as consumers, as drivers, as nondrivers, and as enthusiasts. It focuses on the enormous influence the automobile has had on American culture, from the automotive innovations that have changed our lives to the everyday choices we make about the type of car we drive.

Driving America makes people stop and think about the choices in transportation made throughout history and how those innovations have shaped our landscape today. And that is what we do best here at The Henry Ford. We give context to the past and connect it to today and a possible future. We don't just display vehicles—in this case, some of the most significant cars in American history. We bring the past forward by immersing our visitors in what Henry Ford called the "common genius" of the American people: the stories of ingenuity, resourcefulness, and innovation that have made America the great country it is today.

At every one of our five attractions—Henry Ford Museum, Greenfield Village, The Ford Rouge Factory Tour, The Benson Ford Research Center, and the IMAX Theater—we offer history in a way that is both dynamic and thought provoking. We spark important dialogue. We don't just display artifacts; we make these objects relevant and compelling so that our visitors can see themselves in the stories we present.

Perhaps most importantly, we strive to make our collections accessible through a wide variety of programs and products, such as this book. In the following pages, you'll see some of the cars that Henry Ford himself collected as our first curator and how the collection has grown in stature and significance thanks to the excellent work by our curators today. We do believe this piece is a fitting tribute to the man who put the world on wheels. It is also a magnificent testament to the richness and authenticity of our collections for enthusiasts, historians, and collectors around the world to enjoy.

Patricia E. Mooradian

REFLECTIONS IN THE REAR VIEW MIRROR

By Bob Casey

Senior Curator of Transportation

WHEN I BECAME CURATOR OF TRANSPORTATION AT THE HENRY FORD, I told my mother that the untold hours I spent reading car books and magazines as a boy had not been wasted. I was not squandering my youth; I was preparing for my future career. The remark was true enough, but it glossed over my circuitous path to that career: engineering school, a dozen years in the steel industry, graduate school in history, and three other jobs as a historian before landing at The Henry Ford.

Twenty years after becoming curator, I worked on my last major project—this book. By the time you read this, I will be retired, having turned over the curator's responsibilities to Matt Anderson, who wrote the captions that accompany the photographs in this book. This essay is my last chance to comment on The Henry Ford's automobile collection. It also gives me the opportunity to have a conversation with fellow car enthusiasts about what many of them consider to be a dream job—and to explain why being a curator is not, as some may imagine, like being a kid in a candy store with someone else's money.

One thing that often surprises people about The Henry Ford's car collection is its eclectic nature. What, they ask, does a Bugatti Royale with a custom body from a Munich coachbuilder have in common with a dry-lakes racer with a body adapted from a war-surplus auxiliary fuel tank? Or a 1913 "cycle car" that seats two, one behind the other, with the four-seat winner of a twenty-first century prize for fuel economy? Or, moving beyond the extraordinary, a befinned 1957 De Soto Fireflite hardtop with a 1998 Dodge Ram Quad Cab pickup? Why are such different and often distinctive vehicles brought together under one roof? And why does The Henry Ford collection feature so many makes that aren't Fords?

The answers to these questions can be traced to the answer to another question: Why did the man who said, "History is more or less bunk" create one of the world's great history museums? It turns out that the history Henry Ford thought was bunk was the political and military history he had learned in school, with its emphasis on presidents, senators, and generals. The history that wasn't bunk was the history of everyday people, of their lives and work.

In the 1920s, Ford began collecting physical evidence of that history, including stoves and cooking utensils, sewing machines, tractors, steam engines, machine tools, whole buildings, carriages, locomotives, and, of course, automobiles. He was especially interested in the things he remembered from growing up in the late nineteenth century and things that reflected the pell-mell industrialization in the twentieth. Eventually, he brought his collection together as the educational institution he called the Edison Institute, in honor of his hero Thomas Edison. Today, the Edison Institute is known simply as The Henry Ford, a vast history and technology museum with an outdoor village that reflects three hundred years of American life.

Ford had no interest in restricting the museum's automotive collection to products of the Ford Motor Company. While he did include a number of early-day Fords, he also acquired other low-cost makes, like a Curved Dash Oldsmobile. In addition, he acquired symbols of luxury like a Stevens-Duryea limousine; unsuccessful experiments like a Woods Dual Power hybrid; and history makers like the Packard that was the second car to traverse the United States coast to coast. Henry Ford wanted his collection to reflect epoch-making events as well as trends in automotive marketing, styling, and engineering, such as cars with steam power and electric power.

Seeing no need for employees trained in "museum practice," Ford was his own curator. As a result, for several years after he died in 1947, little was added to the collection. Beginning in the mid-1950s, however, the museum hired professional curators. These curators built upon what was already one of the richest and most varied collections in the world. Following the path the company had laid out, curators responsible for transportation devices acquired vehicles representative of the broad sweep of automotive history. They added classics with custom coachwork and vehicles built for high performance and human derring-do. They also added cars that were important to ordinary men and women: Chevys, Dodges, Nashes, Studebakers, and, yes, Volkswagens and Hondas. These cars ordinarily got used up and thrown away, not put in a museum.

The curators of the transportation collections who came after Henry Ford—Alan Symonds (1956–1960), Les Henry (1960–1977), John Conde (1977–1981), Randy Mason (1981–1992), and this writer (1992–2012)—aimed to build and enrich a collection that represented the ever-changing landscape of American automotive history. That collection has now grown to 260 cars. The one hundred pictured in this book were on display when The Henry Ford opened a new automobile exhibit, *Driving America*, in January 2012.

People often ask me which car is my favorite. I have favorites, of course, but that question is more appropriate for a private collector than for a museum curator. A collector will acquire whatever strikes his or her fancy if it is affordable. There may be a larger agenda—for instance, every Chevy convertible from 1912 to 1975 was the aim of an Iowa enthusiast—or no agenda at all. In contrast, while a curator will inevitably have personal favorites, as I do, he or she must subordinate these to the mission of the institution.

An occupational hazard of the curatorial profession is "gottahavit-itis," the characteristics of which are (1) having an overpowering desire to acquire a particular artifact, and (2) attempting to conjure up any rationale for this acquisition, however far-fetched. I have occasionally been infected with the overpowering desire to acquire a particular artifact but believe I have avoided far-fetched rationales. Henry Ford could collect whatever suited his fancy, but like a good curator, he kept his eye on his broader agenda to include a full range of vehicles reflecting all aspects of American life. That agenda likewise motivated all his successors.

To explain how this has played out over time, let's take a closer look at a dozen of the cars featured in this book, starting with one of the most famous, the 1931 Type 41 Bugatti Royale. Why is a one-of-a-kind French car with a German body in a collection that aims to document America's experience with the automobile? Well, listen to its story.

The original owner was Joseph Fuchs, a wealthy Nuremburg obstetrician who commissioned Ludwig Weinberger to craft a two-door cabriolet on one of Ettore Bugatti's massive Royale chassis. He took delivery in 1932. A year later, Hitler rose to power, and Dr. Fuchs fled to Switzerland. Ultimately, he shipped his Royale to Shanghai and headed there himself. By 1937, Japanese armies were sweeping across China, and Shanghai was no longer a safe haven. With a U.S. visa in hand and his Royale stowed in the hold, Fuchs sailed for North America. Eventually, he drove his Royale across the United States and established a new medical practice in New York City. There, this great car that had been saved over and over from the furies of war succumbed to mundane neglect. Failure to winterize the engine resulted in a cracked block, and by 1943, the once-magnificent Royale was derelict in a Bronx salvage yard.

The Royale was rescued by a longtime admirer, Charles Chayne, who happened to be the chief engineer at Buick. Chayne repaired the engine, changed the color scheme, and modified the steering wheel, seats, and floorboards to accommodate his 6'3" frame. He also replaced the mechanical brakes with hydraulics and installed a new intake manifold set up for four carburetors. After Chayne and his wife, Esther, had enjoyed their Royale for many years, they offered it to the Henry Ford Museum in 1957. Although Henry Ford had died ten years earlier, he certainly would have appreciated the saga of a European classic that spent all but its first few years in the United States and owed its rescue to a top engineer at General Motors, who reconfigured it to suit his own tastes.

If the Bugatti Royale personifies European style and engineering as reinterpreted by an American collector, the 1951 belly tank lakester personifies the ingenuity and passion of American hot rodders. In the 1930s, young Southern Californians enamored with automotive performance began staging events on dry lakebeds in the Mojave Desert, their aim being to clock top speed with electric timers. Souped-up Ford roadsters were the weapon of choice for most competitors. During World War II, one such hot rodder, Bill Burke, spied a cache of teardrop-shaped fuel tanks that were designed for attachment under the wings or fuselage (the "belly") of fighter planes in order to extend their range. These tanks were called "belly tanks" or "drop tanks," because they were designed to be jettisoned when empty. Burke had an inspiration: would not such a tank make a dandy streamlined body for a hot rod that was designed to run at top speed on the dry lakes? Indeed it would, and after the war, Burke built such an aerodynamic creation. It proved much faster than any Ford roadster.

Since the tanks were available for almost nothing, Burke soon had imitators. But ultimately no one was more persistent or successful than Tom Beatty, who fabricated a lakester chassis from chrome-moly "aircraft" tubing. He also knew how to fit four carburetors to a blower from a two-cycle GMC bus engine and bolt it to a flathead (valve-in-block) Mercury V-8 as a supercharger. In 1951, after trailering his creation to a new venue for hot rodders, the Bonneville Salt Flats in Utah, he clocked 188.284 miles per hour. On the dry lakes, he clocked "Top Speed of the Season" for five straight years, 1951 through 1955, and he did it again in 1959 with an Oldsmobile engine.

By 1963, when Tom clocked 252 miles per hour on the salt, the tank was the oldest car at Bonneville and nearing the end of its racing life. By 1965, Tom had retired it to a far corner of his shop. Somehow it survived, first Tom's death, and then getting passed from one new owner to another. Finally, it ended up on the auction block. When I acquired it for The Henry Ford in 2009, it was miraculously close to the condition it was in when Tom last toured the "long course" at Bonneville. Even though it lacks the polish and glamour of the Bugatti, it would be hard to argue that Beatty's creation does not merit a place in the very top of the pantheon of automotive design and engineering.

In 1957, the same year that Tom Beatty set a Bonneville record with flathead power that still stands, and the year before Charles and Esther Chayne donated their Bugatti to the Ford Museum, De Soto produced its flagship Fireflite, as redesigned by Chrysler's head stylist, Virgil Exner. The Fireflite was big and bold, with soaring tailfins, triple-lens taillights, and a 295-horsepower V-8. Nothing better illustrated the desire of many Americans for cars that were flamboyant and powerful. In this era, even Fords, Chevys, and Plymouths were flashy. But the Fireflite went beyond flash. From its four headlights to its pushbutton transmission, the Fireflite screamed modern, and to drive one was to be modern. Magazine and TV ads implied that De Sotos and other Chrysler products were so advanced they actually compressed time. "Suddenly," they proclaimed, "it's 1960."

Ratchet forward forty-odd years to the 1990s, and the world had changed. Automobiles no longer commanded the technological forefront: that honor belonged to high-definition televisions, the Internet, and a hot new device called a GPS. But size still mattered, and Americans were increasingly drawn to supersized pickups, both as symbols of outdoorsy individualism and as safe havens in an increasingly dangerous world. (The laws of physics said that big, heavy vehicles were safer in a crash.) Thus, the best-selling vehicle in the 1990s was the Ford F-150, with Chevy and Dodge pickups exceptionally popular as well. Most of these trucks had an extended cab with a backseat of sorts, but it was cramped. Then in 1998, Dodge came out with a four-door pickup, the Dodge Ram 1500 Quad Cab. With interior styling and ergonomics equal to a passenger car, the Quad Cab was, in effect, a sedan with an enormous trunk.

In the museum's collections, there are two obvious counterpoints to automotive behemoths like the Fireflite and the Quad Cab. One of them is among the oldest cars, made in 1913 by a firm founded by James Scripps-Booth, the heir to the Scripps newspaper-publishing fortune. It's a cycle car powered by a two-cylinder motorcycle engine, and it seats two people as if on a tandem bicycle. The fad for such minicars passed quickly. Most were poorly made, and The Henry Ford's Scripps Booth is among the few that survived to document a forgotten episode in automotive history.

Along with the Scripps-Booth, the collection includes the far more deftly engineered Edison2 from 2010. Edison2 won the $5 million Automotive X Prize offered by the Progressive Insurance Company for a four-passenger VLC (Very Light Car) that could top one hundred miles per gallon on E85 fuel (85 percent ethanol, 15 percent gasoline). Edison2 might be a curatorial gamble—my gamble. It may point in a significant direction for automobile engineering, or like the cycle car, it may be nothing but a dead end: too light and too fussy. Still, it has a one-cylinder turbocharged engine, gets 102.5 miles per gallon, and can reach zero to sixty in fifteen seconds. Would this vehicle be any less worthy of honors for technological ingenuity than the Tom Beatty lakester? I think not (though its long-term significance remains to be seen).

The same holds true for the 2002 Toyota Prius, the first commercially successful internal-combustion/electric hybrid. It may represent the future of the automobile, or it may turn out to be a technological detour. If that is the case, the Prius would have much in common with our 1899 Locomobile and 1907 White steamers and our 1963 Chrysler gas turbine. Still, the Prius may provide enduring symbolism as a car that enabled men or women "to make a statement" about the environment. Fireflites made drivers feel modern; Quad Cabs made them feel rugged; hybrids made them feel virtuous.

Yet hybrid cars have not always been about energy efficiency or clean air. For instance, when the Woods Dual Power was made in 1916, gasoline was cheap and no one cared about exhaust emissions. But the idea of the Dual Power was to combine the best features of internal combustion and electricity. An electric motor provided smooth acceleration up to fifteen miles an hour, and then, when the driver engaged the clutch, the gasoline engine took over for highway speeds. Levers on the steering wheel adjusted the speeds of both motors. Woods literature made operating the car sound simple, but apparently it was not, and by 1918, the company was gone, as were all but a handful of Dual Powers. Thankfully for us, Henry Ford acquired one of the last survivors in 1928.

Ford appreciated the rare, complex, expensive Dual Power for its technology, but he put his own name on cars that were simple, cheap, and consequently, ubiquitous. This was evident in the first Model N Ford, introduced in 1906 and priced at $500. A two-passenger runabout with four cylinders, fifteen horsepower, and a shaft (not chain) drive, the Model N was capable of forty-five miles per hour. Similar-sized competitors from Maxwell, Buick, and Brush could match the Ford in simplicity, or price, but not both. The Model N became America's best-selling car.

When Henry Ford began work on what became the Model T, he started with a Model N chassis, but the product that finally emerged from his Piquette Avenue plant in October 1908 was altogether revolutionary. Today, more than a century after its introduction, "Model T" has come to mean "old-fashioned." But when it was new, the Model T was on the cutting edge of modernity as surely as was the De Soto Fireflite in 1957. The T boasted a one-piece block and removable cylinder head, engineering then found in only a handful of high-priced cars. Extensive use of vanadium alloy steel kept the car's weight down without sacrificing durability, and its power-to-weight ratio was on par with vehicles costing several times more. The frame and suspension were especially suited to the dreadful roads of the time. As innovative production techniques drove the price below $400, the Model T was made affordable to millions of people. America was transformed.

Ironically, the feature of our 1909 Model T touring car that draws the most comments from museum visitors is its color—red. "Weren't all Model Ts black?" people ask. Well, 11.5 million were, but 3.5 million weren't. Colors were available for the first four model years (1909 to 1912) and the last two years of Model T production (1926 to 1927). In 1909, Model T touring cars came in red, green, and occasionally grey, but not black.

The last of our dozen cars is the 1943 Jeep, which actually had much in common with the Model T. Both vehicles were light, nimble, rugged, and versatile. They cost little and were simple to maintain. More than 660,000 were manufactured, many by the Ford Motor Company. For a generation of Europeans, Jeeps symbolized American ingenuity and productive capacity. The "go anywhere, do anything, under any conditions" image remains part of the Jeep mystique to this day. Thus, the driver of a Grand Cherokee cruising to the shopping mall may somehow feel a connection with GIs slogging through war-torn Europe.

Earlier, I said that I have favorites but avoided the question of whether I actually have a favorite. As these will likely be the last words I write about the automotive collection it has been my honor to build and protect, I'll confess: I do have a favorite. It's the 1906 Locomobile race car known as "Old 16." I discovered its story in junior high, in a book beloved by a generation of car enthusiasts, Ken Purdy's *Kings of the Road*. The Locomobile was the first American car to win America's first great international auto race, the Vanderbilt Cup. Jerry Helck, the son of artist and illustrator Peter Helck, offered it to The Henry Ford, unrestored and in running condition. Peter actually saw it race when he was a boy and later fulfilled a dream by acquiring it. Of course, I wanted to jump at the opportunity to acquire the Locomobile, but then I had to ask, Was I just suffering from "gottahavit-itis," or was there a solid case for the historical significance of this car? Well, look at what else happened in 1908, the year Old 16 won the Vanderbilt Cup. In 1908, another American car, a Thomas Flyer, bested German, French, and Italian cars in an epic race from New York City to Paris. In 1908, Wilbur and Orville Wright made the first public demonstrations of their airplane. In 1908, sixteen American battleships—"the Great White Fleet"—completed most of a fourteen-month, around-the-world voyage. In 1908, the Ford Motor Company introduced its revolutionary Model T. And in 1908, William C. Durant put together General Motors, the organization that would supplant Ford as the world's largest automaker.

Old 16's Vanderbilt Cup victory was part of American technology's emergence on the world stage, part of the process that would make the twentieth century "The American Century." Truly, Old 16 was an appropriate addition to our collection, if for no other reason than to serve as an emblem for so many other events that took place in 1908. No far-fetched rationale necessary.

Recounting the stories of Old 16 and the other eleven cars is a bit like participating in an archeological dig, slicing through the layers of automotive history from 2009 back to 1906. Indeed, The Henry Ford's entire automobile collection can be likened to artifacts dug from a very large slice through auto history, revealing a bottom layer that dates to 1865. Each vehicle speaks volumes about the time and place in which it was created, yet each is related to the vehicles in the layers above and below it. But archeological digs only look backward in time from a particular vantage point. For the museum's curators, the vantage point is always changing, moving forward in time. Matt Anderson and his successors will constantly encounter new technologies, new consumer wants and needs, new fashions, new government regulations, and new political considerations that will affect the automobiles of the future. The challenge—and the fun—of their job will be sifting through the scores of available vehicles to pick the ones that say the most about those times. Whether those vehicles are one-offs or just one of millions, they will be key elements in the ever-changing story of America, whose material culture is the glory of The Henry Ford.

Bob Casey

THE ROAD AHEAD

BY MATT ANDERSON

Curator of Transportation

L IKE MOST BOYS, I WAS FASCINATED WITH CARS FROM AN EARLY AGE. Friday nights spent with *The Dukes of Hazzard* gave way to Saturday nights at the local dirt track, ultimately culminating in a driver's license and a used 1987 Plymouth Horizon. The 1980s weren't always the best of times for gearheads. My parents' generation had car movies like *Goldfinger* and *Bullitt*; mine had *Roger & Me*. The Big Three weren't so much trying to out-style or out-gadget each other. Some years, they were merely trying to survive. But there were always exciting cars—for instance, the Dodge Viper, the Ford Taurus SHO, and the Corvette ZR1—to fire a boy's imagination and instill a lifelong interest in the automobile's evolving role in American culture.

As I begin my work as Curator of Transportation at The Henry Ford, I find myself both invigorated by the museum's unparalleled collection and anxious at the responsibility of building it for the next generation. Bob Casey and his predecessors have done an outstanding job of assembling a collection that is concise yet broad enough to reflect America's ever-changing relationship with the automobile—a phenomenon now well into its second century. Their skillful curatorial judgments have provided a sound model for me to follow.

Since I've joined the museum, people have asked me which vehicles the museum will collect in the years ahead. It's impossible to answer that question specifically. Too many variables go into an acquisition. First and foremost, we evaluate the car's historical significance and impact. Nearly as important are the stories associated with that particular vehicle: Who owned it? How was it used? Where did it go? Other considerations include the car's physical condition, the costs involved in transport and maintenance, and the museum's pending exhibit needs.

In lieu of naming specific vehicles, I will suggest three remarkable changes to our car culture that are currently playing out. Each seems worthy of documentation, and each could be told through a new vehicle added to the museum's collection.

The first change is arguably the most dramatic in automotive history. If twentieth-century improvements like electric starters, automatic transmissions, and power steering eased the driver's burden, then the twenty-first century is poised to remove the driver from the equation altogether. We already have cars that automatically adjust cruise control settings, warn distracted drivers, and park. It is only a matter of time before we have completely autonomous automobiles—cars capable of sensing their environments, plotting their routes, and driving to their destinations. "Driverless" cars promise everything from allowing us to work (or nap) during our commutes to reducing our need for directional road signs. They also have the potential to save lives by decreasing accidents. When self-driving cars finally appear, there will be a place for one in The Henry Ford.

The second change is something few people would have predicted twenty, or even ten, years ago. The United States may be on the verge of energy independence. The emerging solution lies not in alternative fuel sources but in more efficient harvesting of our existing fossil fuel reserves. It's far too soon to say that this method, hydraulic fracturing (fracking) of shale oil, is our salvation. To be sure, oil will still run out someday, and growing demand will keep gasoline prices high. Likewise, the fracking process brings new environmental concerns. But the United States sits atop the largest shale oil reserves in the world. If this oil can be harvested safely and profitably, then reports of the internal combustion engine's imminent death are greatly exaggerated. If anything, history suggests that our cars will get bigger and thirstier if gas prices fall.

Third, solid statistics and anecdotal evidence both suggest that the Millennial Generation (born roughly between the early 1980s and the early 2000s) is indifferent toward the automobile. In a nation where "youth" and "car" have been nearly synonymous for a century, this comes as quite a shock. But there are logical reasons behind the trend. New regulations mean that obtaining a driver's license isn't the same teenage rite of passage it once was. In many states, young drivers receive restricted licenses that prevent them from traveling at night or carrying multiple friends. Full driving privileges aren't granted until age eighteen. Money is another issue. For many young adults, the global economic crisis that started in 2008 has put auto ownership out of reach. It's hard to justify monthly car payments when student loan payments are high and job prospects are low. Finally, cars simply seem to have lost their cool cachet. Teenagers and twenty-somethings are more likely to lust over smartphones and tablet computers than hatchbacks—hybrid or otherwise. It may be, too, that increasing sophistication and automation are taking some of the fun out of driving. Engines are too complicated for even routine maintenance to be done at home, much less the hot rodding of years past. Drivers are less engaged with their cars, both under the hood and behind the wheel. Manufacturers are working hard to lure Millennials with vehicles that are affordable, enjoyable, and tech-savvy, but it's a challenge.

We will know, perhaps sooner than we think, whether these three examples represent lasting changes in our relationship with the automobile or are mere historical anomalies that come and go. There are cars from each category in The Henry Ford's collection, and an autonomous sedan or a social media–ready compact would surely fit into the mix. It is the curator's job to determine which cars best document these changes. Should the driverless car be represented with an early prototype, the first commercial model, or the first model to gain widespread public acceptance? Should the Millennials' story be told with an example of the cars that failed to capture their imaginations or a model designed specifically for their market? The decision will depend on what is available, which parts of those stories we choose to emphasize, and how we plan to exhibit the vehicles.

Whatever the automobile's future brings, The Henry Ford will document it. As you'll see on the following pages, it's been an exciting trip so far . . . and we're only getting started.

THE GALLERY

1951 BEATTY BELLY TANK LAKESTER LAND SPEED RACE CAR

The quest for land speed records is as old as the automobile itself, but a traditional car
body creates speed-robbing drag. Tom Beatty and other postwar hot rodders found a clever
solution in the aerodynamic belly fuel tanks developed for P–38 Lightning airplanes. The tanks
were just big enough to accommodate an engine, running gear, and a driver. Beatty drove
this Belly Tank Lakester to 243.438 miles per hour on Utah's Bonneville Salt Flats,
earning records and acclaim through the 1950s and early 1960s.

1915 BREWSTER TOWN LANDAULET

Brewster & Company, which had built refined carriages since 1810, moved into upmarket
automobiles in 1915. Early models featured a distinctive oval radiator that called to mind a
steam locomotive as readily as a carriage. The Great Depression killed the company, but
not before Cole Porter immortalized it in his song "You're the Top," writing,
"You're a Ritz hot toddy, you're a Brewster body. . . ."

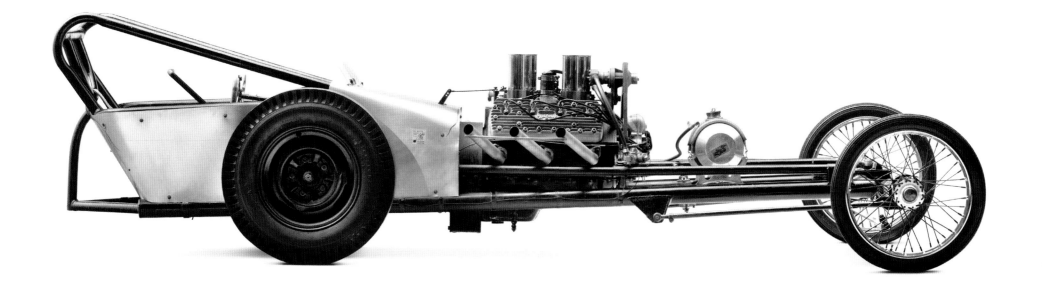

1960 BUCK & THOMPSON SLINGSHOT DRAGSTER

Drag racing is an original American pastime and the purest test of acceleration. Drivers
have faced off in street races since the dawn of motoring, but the establishment of the National
Hot Rod Association legitimized the sport in 1951. Sam Buck and Bob Thompson built their
first racer in 1958 and made names for themselves on the amateur circuit. Their 1960
Slingshot Dragster won championships at Cordova, Illinois, and Bakersfield, California,
during its four-year career. The driver sat at the very back of the car behind the
rear axle—like a rock in a slingshot.

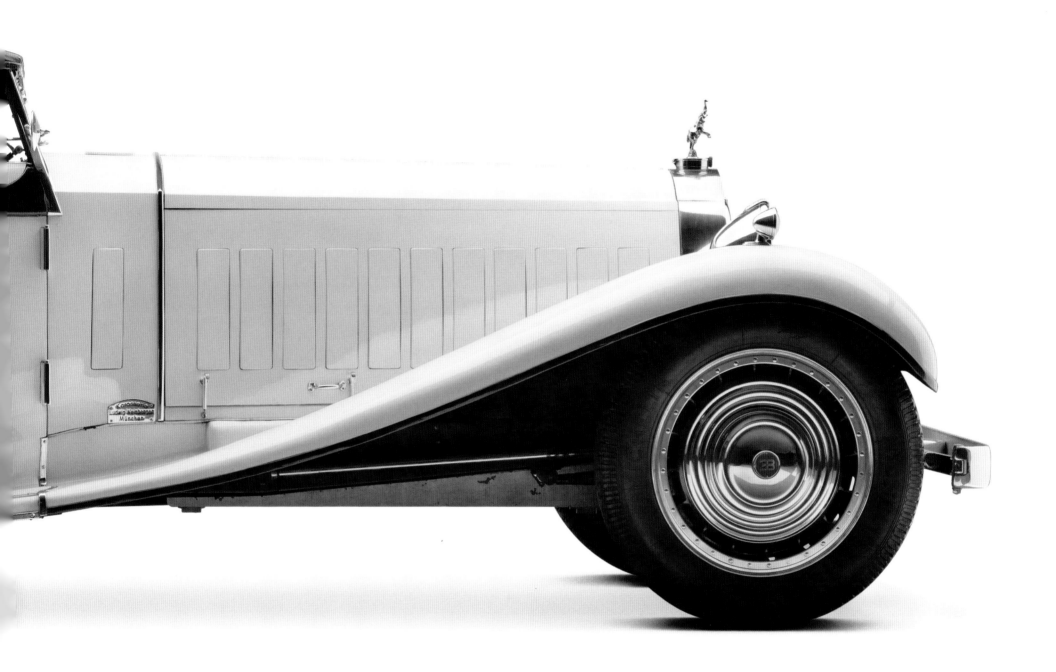

1931 BUGATTI TYPE 41 ROYALE CONVERTIBLE

These might be the most extraordinary automobiles ever built. Ettore Bugatti put
everything he knew—and he knew a lot—about performance and styling into his Type 41
cars. Among the technical features was an aluminum engine block. Design touches included
front and rear fenders that seemed to meld into continuous curves. Only seven Type 41s were
built, including one prototype. Each was individually handcrafted, and no two were alike.
Bugatti managed to sell only three, but one suspects that sales were never the point.

1963 BUICK RIVIERA COUPE

After several years of having the personal luxury field to itself, Thunderbird got competition from Buick's Riviera. The aggressive front end had razor-edge fenders that suggested both speed and sophistication, a dramatic contrast to Buick's boxier offerings. Creature comforts like automatic transmission, adjustable steering, and power windows were standard, as was the powerful, 401-cubic-inch engine.

1959 Cadillac Eldorado Biarritz Convertible

If any vehicle captured the design excesses of 1950s American cars, it was the 1959 Cadillac.
The car was a direct response to Chrysler's exciting "Forward Look" designs. The jet motif
was in full flower, from the intake-like parking lamps on the front bumper to the flame-tip
taillights on the fins. And "wide" didn't even begin to describe the grille, which
wrapped around to the fenders.

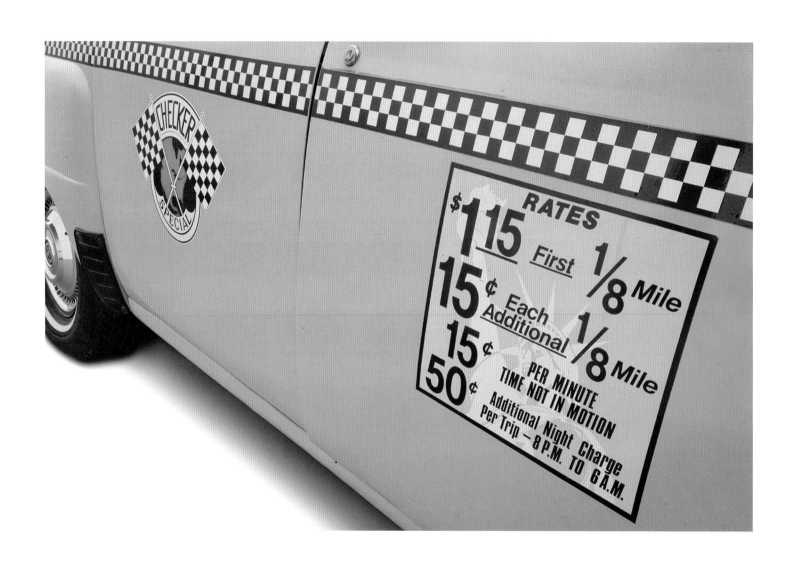

1981 CHECKER MARATHON TAXICAB

It won't win any prizes for style, but Checker's iconic Marathon cab does embody a certain design aesthetic. This car was built for endurance. The frame was heavily reinforced, the fenders bolted on and off for easy replacement, and the front and rear bumpers were interchangeable. The car's appearance was also intended to be as timeless as possible. Checker avoided annual style updates, and one is hard pressed to tell a 1960 model from its 1982 counterpart.

1915 CHEVROLET ROYAL MAIL ROADSTER

Billy Durant took aim at Ford's Model T with his Chevrolet line. Priced below $1,000,
the Royal Mail was more expensive than a Ford, but it boasted technical improvements
like an electric starter, overhead valves, and electric headlights. The Chevy also had a
dash of flair in its long hood, swept cowling, and short rear deck.

1955 CHEVROLET CORVETTE ROADSTER

While the 1953 Corvette's look wowed Motorama crowds, its performance left something
to be desired. The six-cylinder engine and two-speed automatic transmission didn't exactly
scream "sports car." But the 1955 model offered an optional V-8 and a three-speed manual
shift, lending power and credibility. Through movies, television shows, and countless
owners—or those who merely dream of owning one—the Corvette has acquired
a lasting mystique as America's sports car.

1955 CHEVROLET BEL AIR HARDTOP

In the mid-1950s, Chevrolet shed its stodgy image and made a play for the youth market.
The result was a revelation. The 1955 Chevy combined great looks with power and agility.
The egg crate grille echoed Ferrari, while the notched beltline defied convention.
The optional V-8, available in a Chevrolet for the first time since 1918, justified
its nickname: "The Hot One."

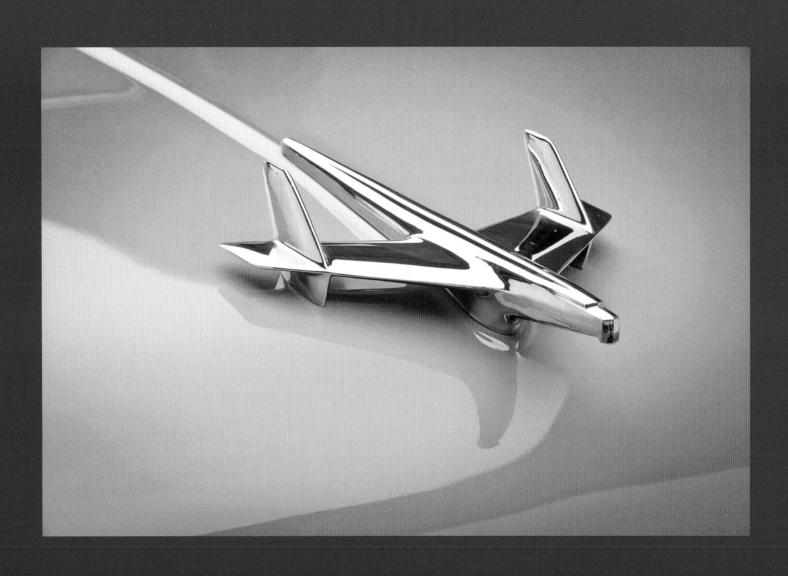

1956 Chevrolet Bel Air Convertible

Contrasts between Chevrolet's 1955 and 1956 models reveal how a few tweaks can alter
the overall feel of a car. The flatter hood and two-tone "speedlines" along the side gave the
1956 a lower, longer feel. The new taillight treatment emphasized chrome over clean lines.
And the full-width grille gave the impression of greater breadth. The 1956 Bel Air
was still a beautiful car, but it was decidedly busier than its predecessor.

1960 CHEVROLET CORVAIR SEDAN

It was the year of the compact. In 1960, Ford and Plymouth introduced scaled-down versions
of traditional sedans, yet Chevrolet's innovative Corvair was unlike any other American car.
The rear-mounted, air-cooled engine opened up the car's interior—but it also compromised
handling. Chevy corrected the problems, but not before Ralph Nader's book *Unsafe at
Any Speed* branded the Corvair as dangerous in the public's mind.

1924 CHRYSLER TOURING CAR

Walter P. Chrysler left the railroad industry to join Buick in 1910. He ascended to the
presidency, but he grew tired of working for the mercurial Billy Durant and left to helm
the flailing Willys-Overland Company in 1919. Chrysler next rescued Maxwell Motor
Corporation, where he introduced a car bearing his name in 1924. The Chrysler Touring
Car was the first medium-priced American car with a high performance engine and
could top out at an easy seventy miles per hour. The car was a hit, and by 1925,
Chrysler Corporation had absorbed the Maxwell company.

1956 Chrysler 300-B Stock Car

Carl Kiekhaefer brought a new level of professionalism to NASCAR in the mid-1950s. His drivers and crew members wore uniforms; his cars rode in enclosed transporters rather than open trailers; and his teams rehearsed their pit stops between races. While Chrysler itself eschewed racing, Kiekhaefer embraced the company's 300-letter series, which combined luxury with high performance. In 1956, his teams claimed twenty-two wins with the big 300s.

1963 Chrysler Turbine Sedan

In a bold experiment, Chrysler put forty-six turbine-powered cars in the hands of 203 select motorists over a two-year period. Participants raved about the car's smooth operation and low maintenance but criticized its slow acceleration and poor fuel economy. After tightening government emissions standards led Chrysler to refocus its engineering efforts on piston engines, the turbine program ended.

1973 CHRYSLER NEWPORT SEDAN

While Chevrolet, Ford, and AMC introduced subcompacts in 1970, Chrysler continued to focus on full-size models. In fact, Chrysler's Newport got even bigger, going from 224 inches long for the 1972 model to 230 inches the next year. When the 1973 oil embargo crisis tripled gas prices, the industry's modest move toward smaller cars became an all-out stampede. Chrysler's miscalculation contributed to the company's near-bankruptcy in 1979.

1901 COLUMBIA VICTORIA

Like bicycles and motorcycles of the same name, Columbia automobiles were first built
by the Pope Manufacturing Company in collaboration with the Electric Vehicle Company.
Electric Vehicle Company held George Selden's tenuous 1895 patent on the internal
combustion automobile. Electric Vehicle thrived on royalties from other carmakers until
Henry Ford's legal challenge nullified the patent in 1911. The 1901 Victoria placed
the driver behind the passengers—an unusual arrangement for a car.

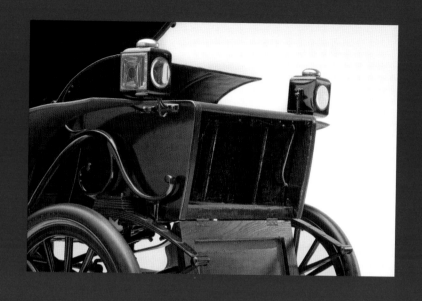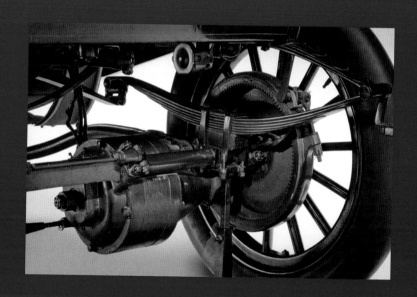

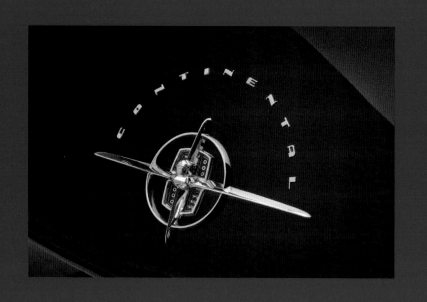

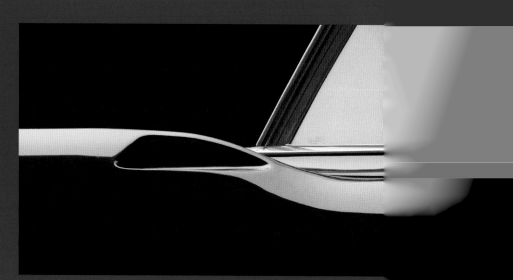

1956 Continental Mark II Sedan

With the Mark II, Ford aspired to build nothing less than the highest quality automobile on the market. Suppliers' parts were checked and re-checked, factory components were tested and re-tested, and assembly workers were told to report even the slightest defect. The Mark II also benefited from an understated elegance—a stark contrast to the era's chrome confections. It was a magnificent car, and at $9,966 dollars, it had a price to match.

1980 COMUTA-CAR ELECTRIC RUNABOUT

The electric Comuta-Car was among the more unorthodox responses to the 1970s oil
crises. Introduced as CitiCar in 1974, it reappeared under new ownership in 1978. Although
some four thousand units were built, the car was doomed by its slow speed, which was
insufficient for interstate highway travel; increasingly strict federal crash standards;
and, most of all, falling gas prices.

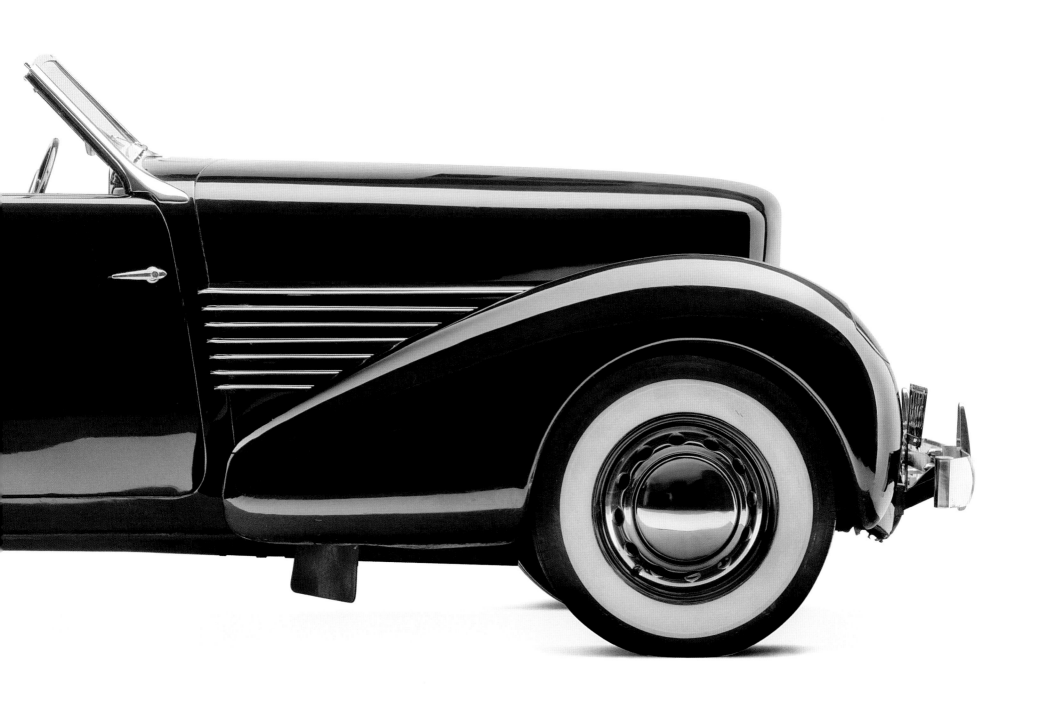

1937 CORD 812 CONVERTIBLE

Form and function blended magnificently in the Cord 812. The car's low profile resulted
from the then-unusual front-wheel-drive arrangement, eliminating the need for a driveshaft
tunnel. The wraparound grille and "coffin" nose concealed a gearbox mounted in front
of the engine. And the gearbox's location prompted an electro-vacuum shifter, which
in turn complemented the dashboard's modern appearance.

1957 CORNELL-LIBERTY CONCEPT SAFETY CAR

As power and speed increased, so did fatal accidents. Serious safety research began in the 1950s.
Cornell Aeronautical Laboratory incorporated more than sixty safety improvements into this
nonoperational concept car. Interior surfaces were rounded and padded. The steering wheel and
column, notorious for impaling drivers in head-on collisions, was replaced by sliding handles.
The sliding dashboard moved tight against the driver, while seat belts kept passengers secure.
Automakers ultimately adapted many of these innovations for production vehicles.

1951 CROSLEY HOTSHOT ROADSTER

Appliance magnate Powel Crosley, Jr., launched Crosley Motors just in time for World War II. Fortunately for Crosley, military contracts gave the company sound finances, and the war's end brought eager buyers. The playful Hotshot joined Crosley's small sedans, coupes, and wagons in 1949. Though lacking in creature comforts, the Hotshot was a performer that could break one hundred miles per hour. Crosley's commitment to small cars, however, was out of tune with the American market. His auto company folded in 1952.

1957 De Soto Fireflite Hardtop

Designer Virgil Exner rejuvenated Chrysler's lineup with a companywide makeover
in 1955. The "Forward Look" emphasized long lines and bright colors, drawing inspiration
from *au courant* jet aircraft. Even the dashboards, with pushbuttons in place of gearshift
levers, were more cockpit than driver's seat. Exner's 1957 models also featured the
jet theme's ultimate expression: tail fins.

1914 DETROIT ELECTRIC MODEL 47 BROUGHAM

Like many early automakers, Detroit Electric descended from a carriage works. The
company moved from Port Huron, Michigan, to Detroit in 1895 and built its first electric car
in 1907. The clean, quiet vehicles were well suited to urban driving, but gasoline soon became
the dominant power source. Detroit Electric turned to commercial vehicles in the 1920s,
and when the company closed in 1938, it was America's last surviving maker of electric
automobiles. This particular car was Clara Ford's personal vehicle.

1978 DODGE OMNI SEDAN

Chrysler became the first American manufacturer to emulate European subcompact
designs when it introduced the Dodge Omni and twin Plymouth Horizon in 1978. The
cars were small, but engineers maximized space with a transverse engine/front-wheel-drive
arrangement in the front and a hatchback in the rear. Critical and commercial successes,
these subcompacts put beleaguered Chrysler on the road to recovery.

1998 DODGE RAM QUAD CAB PICKUP TRUCK

Long the domain of farmers and contractors, pickup trucks were mainstream by the
1990s. Growing sales for the Ford F-150 and Chevy Silverado prompted Dodge to redesign
its Ram for 1994. Under its brawny exterior were refinements more typical of a sedan.
The 1998 model added optional rear doors that made the rear seat more accessible and
turned the pickup into a viable substitute for the family car.

1931 DUESENBERG MODEL J CONVERTIBLE VICTORIA

Fred and August Duesenberg had years of proven success in racing and commercial
production when E. L. Cord brought them into his industrial empire in 1926. Cord's
instructions to the brothers were simple: build the world's finest automobile. The resulting
Model J merited every superlative showered upon it. It was beautiful, it was powerful, and
it was expensive. But the Great Depression, along with Fred's untimely death in 1932,
hastened the end of production in 1937.

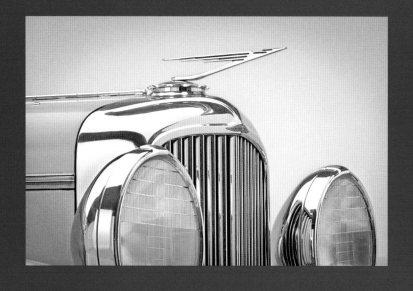

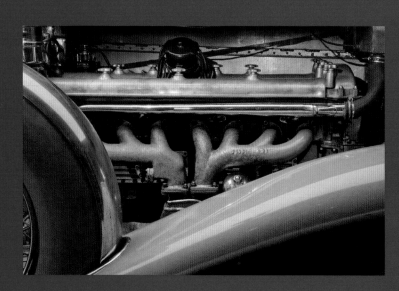

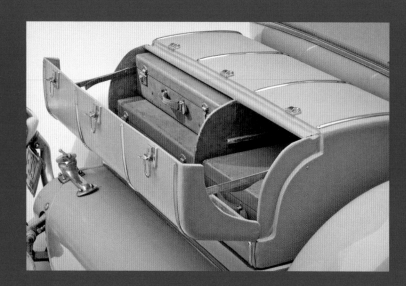

1896 DURYEA RUNABOUT

Brothers Charles and Frank Duryea inaugurated the American automobile industry with their 1896 Runabout, the first series-produced automobile made in the United States. Only thirteen were built, but they were *copies*—identical cars as opposed to singular prototypes or custom orders made on demand. The Duryeas' firm lasted just three years, but its place in history is secure. Of those thirteen pioneering cars, this is the only known survivor.

1899 DURYEA TRAP

The Duryeas parted ways as business partners in 1898. Charles carried on with the
Duryea Trap, a three-wheeled design. Today, it is easy to label the Trap as unconventional,
but in 1899, there were no conventions in automobile design. The Trap was inspired
by the curving lines of the Victoria-style carriage.

2010 EDISON2 CONCEPT CAR

The Edison2 suggested dramatic new directions for the American automobile when it won the 2010 Progressive Insurance Automotive X PRIZE. The contest called for a car capable of taking four adults two hundred miles on a single tank of gas while averaging one hundred miles per gallon. Lightweight but conventional materials and an exceptionally aerodynamic design gave the Edison2 a range of six hundred miles and an efficiency rating of 102.5 miles per gallon.

1958 EDSEL CITATION HARDTOP

It's easy to point fingers at that grille, but in truth, the Edsel was damned by Ford's overpraise. The company's massive marketing blitz promised "the newest thing on wheels." What drivers got instead was a fairly pedestrian design with engineering and styling that borrowed from existing Ford products. Even the splashier features, like the "Teletouch" pushbutton transmission, seemed more like gimmicks than true innovation.

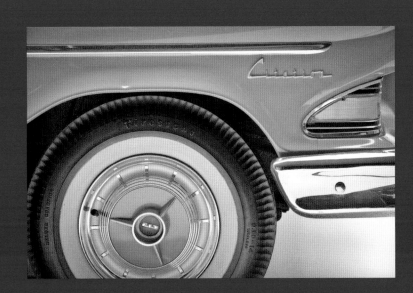

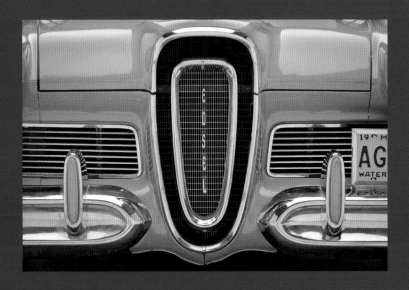

1924 Essex Coach Sedan

In 1922, when Essex introduced an enclosed car that cost only slightly more than open
models, year-round driving became practical, and the popularity of touring cars came to an
end. The Hudson Motor Car Company had formed the Essex Motor Car Company in 1918
to produce smaller, moderately-priced cars to complement Hudson's larger Super-Six.
Essex ceased to be a separate company in 1922 and simply became a Hudson make
until the Essex name was retired in 1932.

1896 Quadricycle Runabout

Henry Ford's first automobile was the quintessential home-built contraption. Its two cylinders were made from a steam engine's exhaust pipe, the seat came from a buggy, and its wheels were those of a bicycle. There were few ready-made parts and limited published information on others' experiments, so Ford learned by doing. He took his first successful drive on June 4, 1896, after two and a half years of planning, building, and rebuilding.

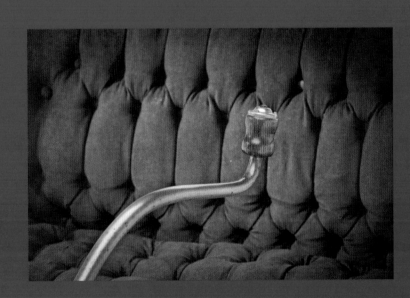

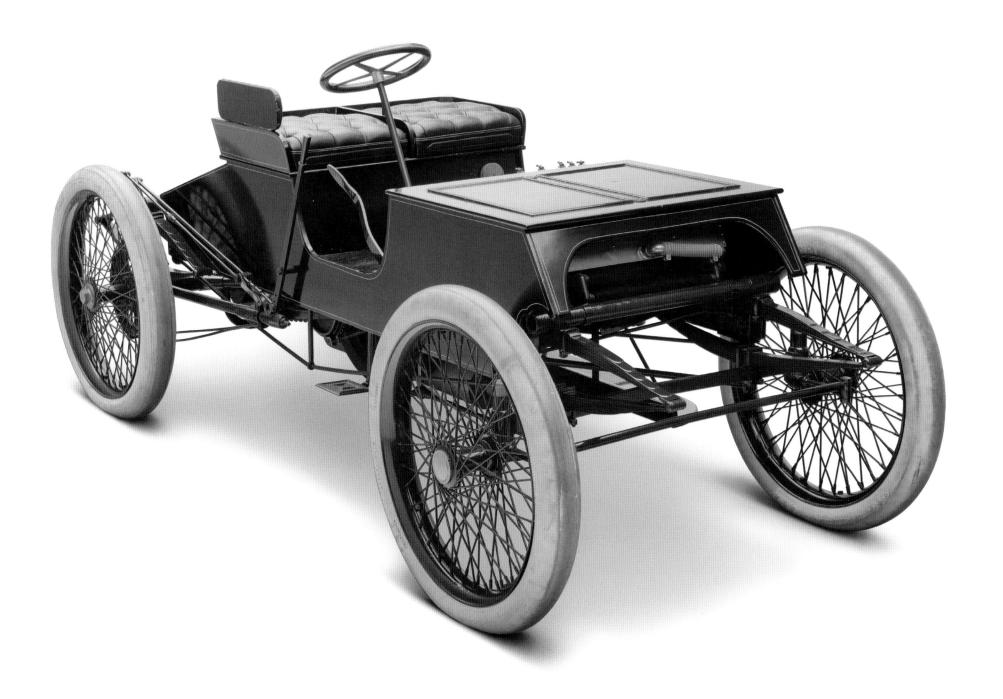

1901 FORD "SWEEPSTAKES" RACE CAR

It's the stuff of legend: a novice underdog beats a renowned champion. After his first auto
company failed, Henry Ford looked to restore his reputation through racing. Ford built
"Sweepstakes" and drove it against Alexander Winton on October 10, 1901. Winton, then
among the best-known racers in the United States, took an early lead but fell behind at
the eighth lap. Henry Ford's victory and the resulting publicity encouraged Detroit
financiers to back his second company.

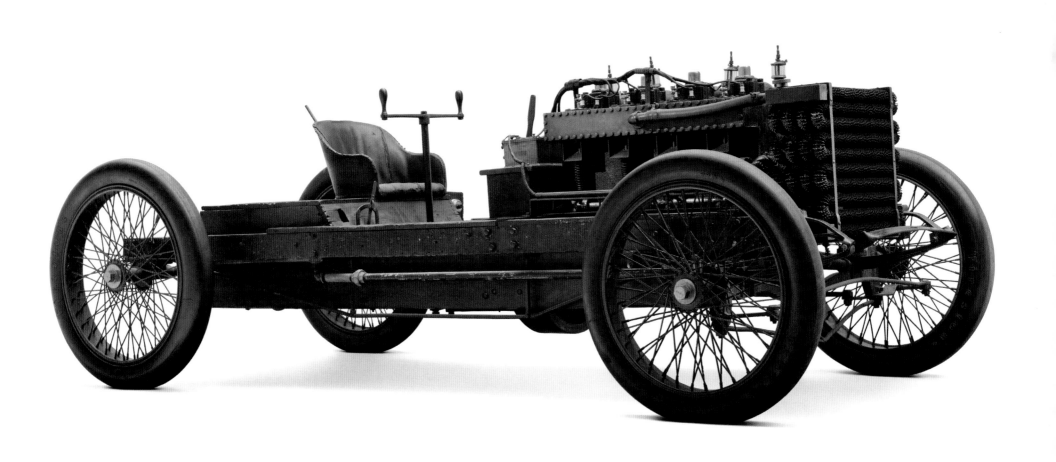

1902 Ford "999" Race Car

With his second race car, the "999," Henry Ford created a monster that was too powerful even for him. The car, with its massive 1,156-cubic-inch engine, carried only essential equipment and had no exhaust system, no transmission, and no protection for the driver. Ford sold the car to his business partner Tom Cooper, who in turn hired bicycle racer Barney Oldfield to drive. Oldfield and "999" proved a winning team. Barney Oldfield became motorsport's first superstar, while Henry Ford secured his reputation as a builder of quality automobiles.

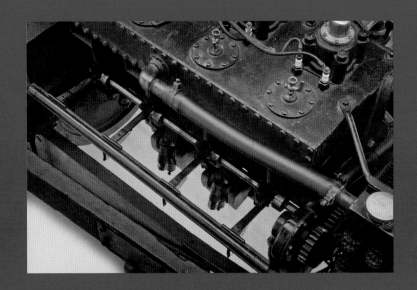

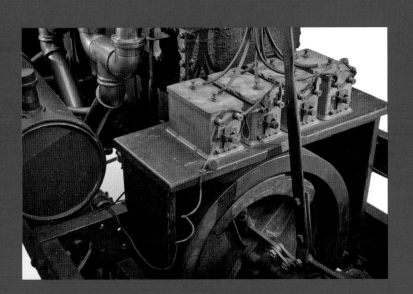

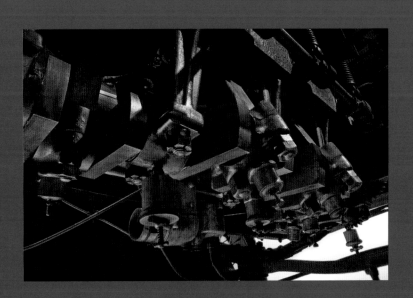

1903 FORD MODEL A RUNABOUT

For Henry Ford, the third time was the charm. After two unsuccessful attempts at commercial automaking, he established Ford Motor Company in 1903. The firm's first product, sensibly called the Model A, was conventional for the day, with a two-cylinder engine mounted under the seat and its rear wheels driven by a chain.

1905 FORD MODEL B TOURING CAR

Ford's Model B was a significant technological advance over the Model A. The B's longitudinal
engine sat up front, and power reached the rear wheels through a driveshaft rather than a
simple chain. The car also was a lot more expensive thanks to some of Henry Ford's financial
backers, who favored pricey cars to generate profits. Ford, however, had other ideas.

1906 FORD MODEL N RUNABOUT

Henry Ford had to buy out his backers, but he got his way. His vision called for building
small, inexpensive cars and selling them in large quantities to make money. The Model N,
a solid car that cost less than the popular, curved-dash Oldsmobile, was very much
in keeping with that idea. It proved to be a sales success.

1908 Ford Model S Roadster

The use of common platforms, in which a single chassis is the basis for several different cars,
is a time-tested practice. Ford's Model N was the foundation for two somewhat upmarket cars:
the Model R, which featured running boards, additional trim, and a mechanical lubricator;
and the Model S, which added a single-seat tonneau to the package. The Model S was
Ford's last American car with driver controls on the right.

1909 Ford Model T Touring Car

Henry Ford finally crafted his ideal car with the Model T. Here was a rugged yet reliable automobile suitable for quantity production. The T wasn't fully realized at its introduction, though. The first 2,500 carried a gear-driven water pump instead of the simpler thermo–syphon cooling system adopted later. Rarer still, the first one thousand or so Model Ts, such as this one, engaged their reverse gears by means of a lever rather than a floor pedal.

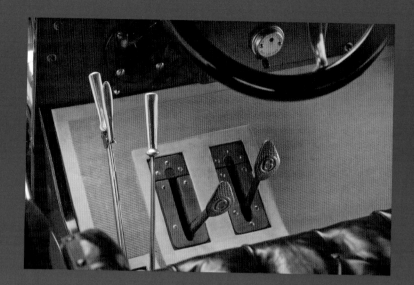

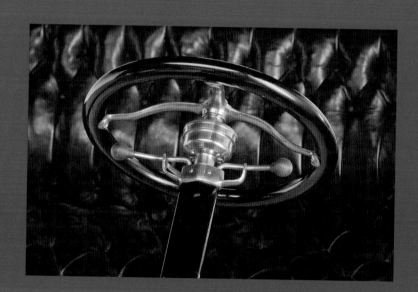

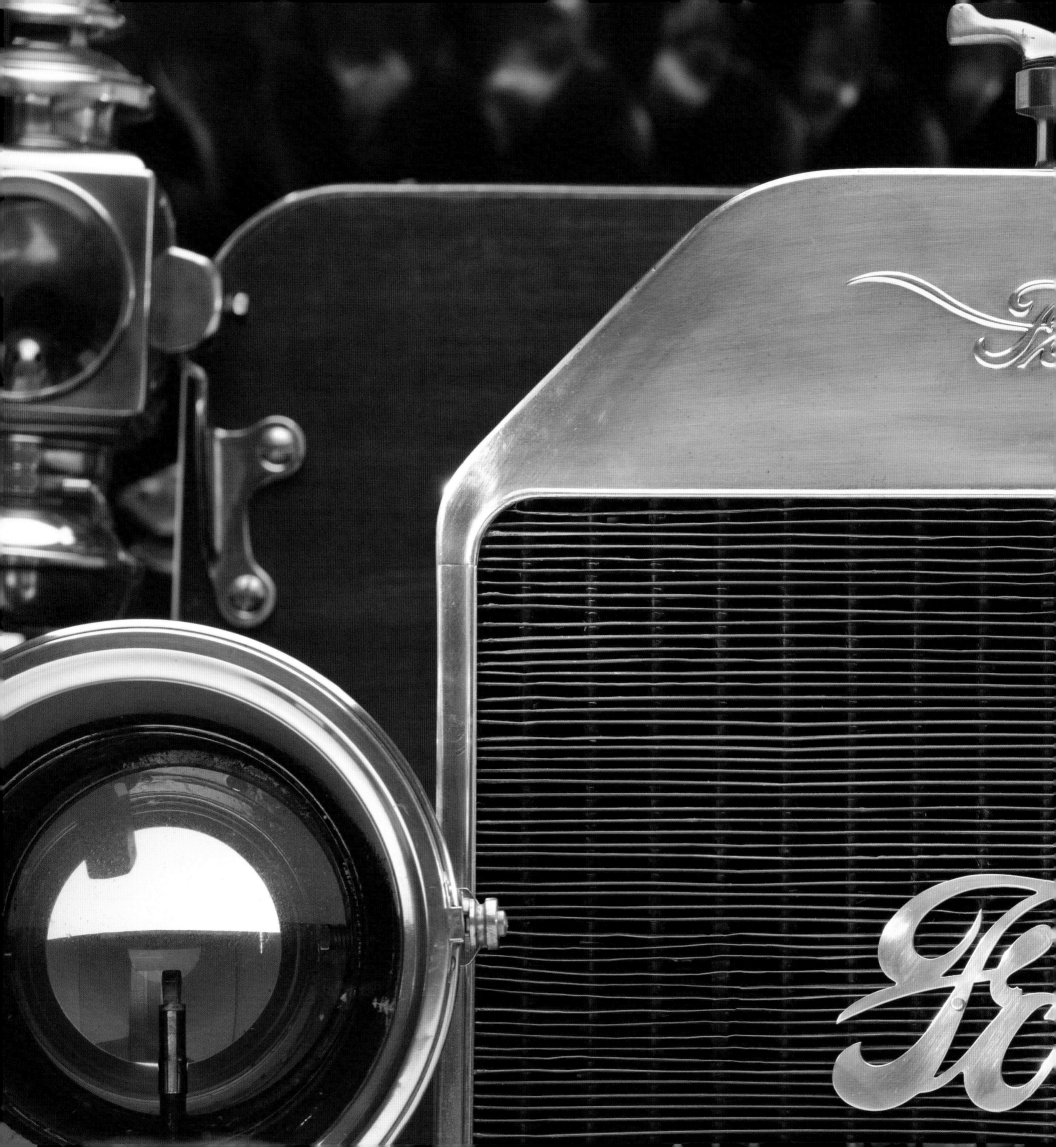

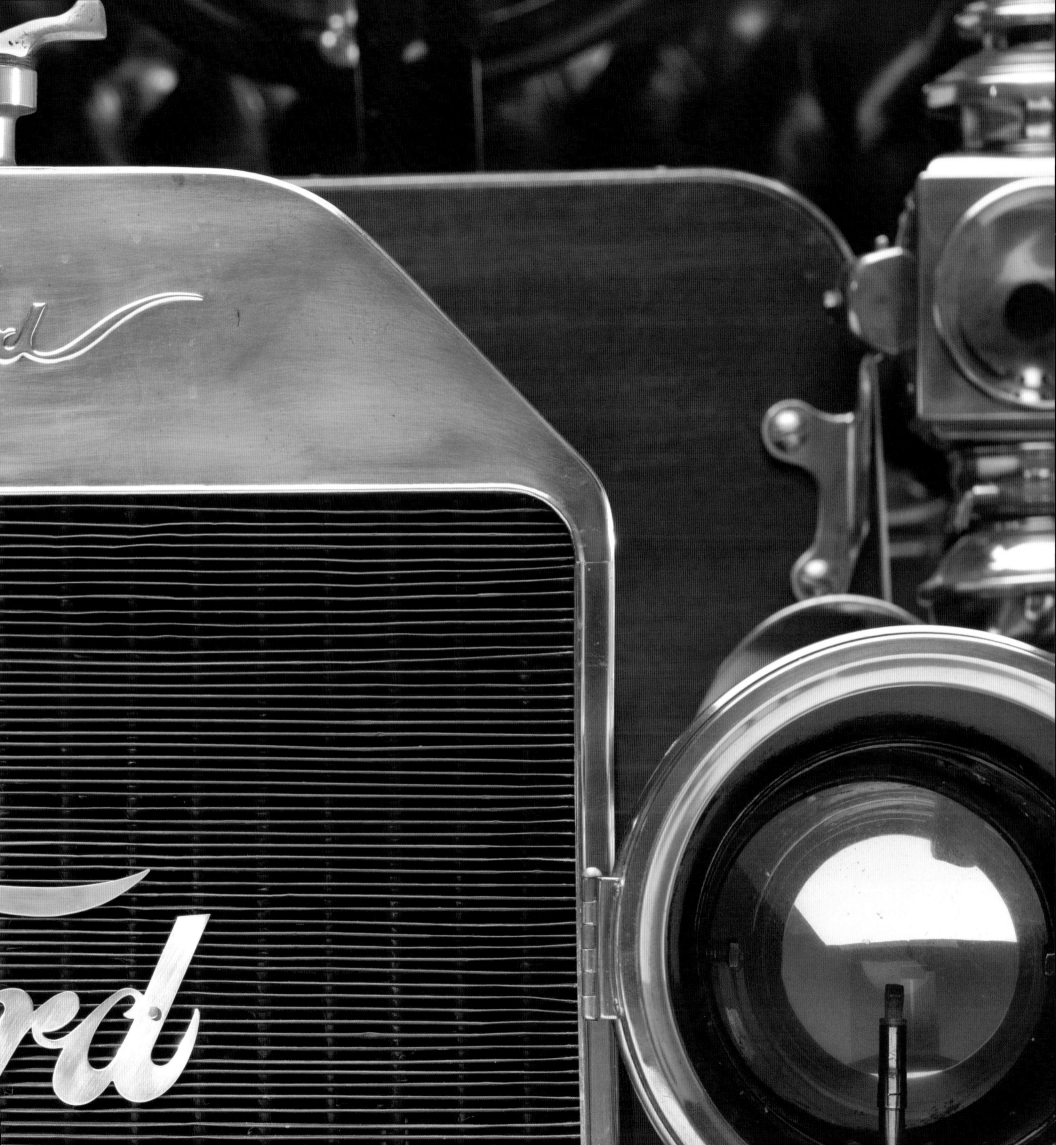

1914 FORD MODEL T TOURING CAR

The 1914 Model T perfectly reflected Henry Ford's automaking philosophy: build a
quality automobile as inexpensively as possible. By 1914, all Fords were built on an assembly
line, which almost eliminated skilled labor. Workers quickly tired of their repetitive tasks,
but Ford reduced turnover—and turned his employees into middle-class
customers—by paying them five dollars a day.

1919 FORD MODEL T SEDAN

The Model T's fundamental design remained static over its nineteen-year life, but scores
of smaller changes took place. Some incorporated mechanical improvements, some responded
to growing consumer demands, and some simply reduced costs. The 1919 sedans were the
first to offer electric starters and demountable tire rims. These features cost extra on a Ford,
which kept the base price low, even though they were standard on other makes.

1930 FORD MODEL A TOURING CAR

Declining sales and his own staff's pleas finally convinced Henry Ford to retire the Model T.
Production ceased, and most workers were laid off for six months while the company replaced
T-specific tools and dies with new equipment to build the Model A. For all of the company's
challenges, the Model A was a success. It was faster and more mechanically advanced than the
Model T. Thanks to contributions from Edsel Ford, it was decidedly more stylish, too.

1932 FORD ROADSTER

Hot rodding originated in Southern California's dry lakebeds, where drivers raced
modified cars in the 1930s. Enthusiast magazines and clubs made the fad more mainstream
by the 1950s—and Ford's 1930s roadsters were well suited to the hobby. They were
lightweight, mechanically simple, and not antique but merely used. The plentiful cars
sold for pennies on the dollar, well within a teenager's reach.

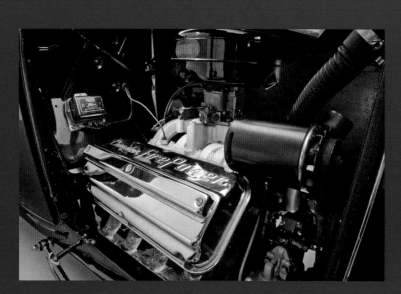

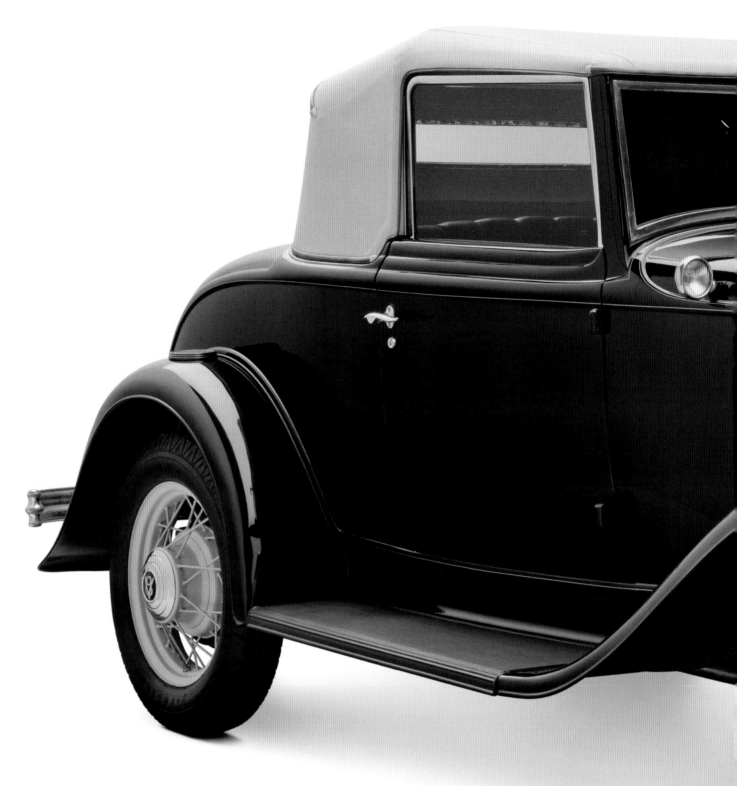

1932 Ford V-8 Cabriolet

The 1932 Ford was the last automobile designed with direct input from Henry Ford.
The car was attractive, but its real innovation was under the hood. Ford insisted on having
an affordable V-8 engine to upstage Chevrolet's low-priced six-cylinder model. He achieved
this by casting the crankcase and cylinders as a single unit, which reduced production costs.
The venerable engine stayed in production until 1953.

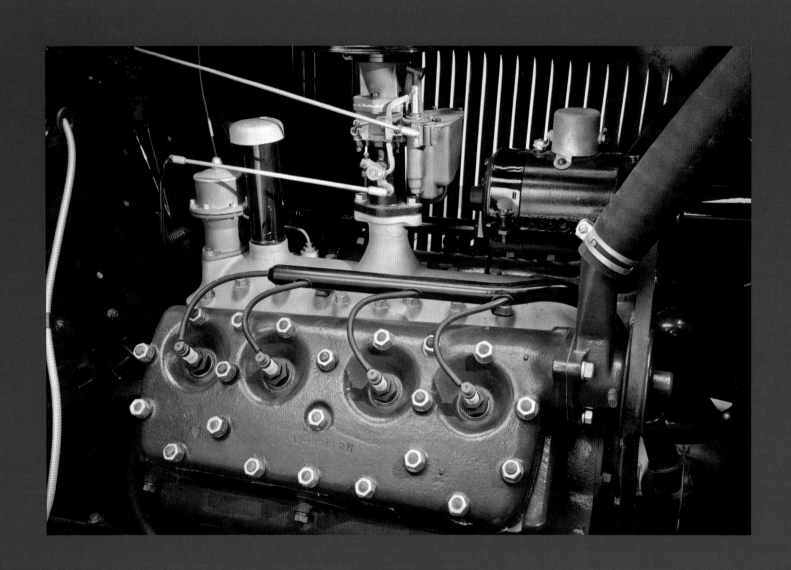

1939 FORD DeLUXE CONVERTIBLE COUPE

While varying levels of style and prestige were offered between the Ford, Mercury, and
Lincoln divisions, by 1939 there were options within the Ford brand itself. Buyers choosing
a DeLuxe model paid more, but they received a car with a sharply pointed hood, a rakishly
low grille, and teardrop headlights mounted directly into the front fenders. Ford's 1939
models also were the company's first to be equipped with hydraulic brakes.

1949 Ford Tudor Sedan

To the modern viewer, the 1949 Ford looks rather ordinary. But that's precisely the point. When it was introduced, the car's "envelope" body, with its integral fenders and smooth slab sides, represented a complete change in the design conventions that had been in place since before the Model T. The clean look proved so popular that it became an industry standard still used today.

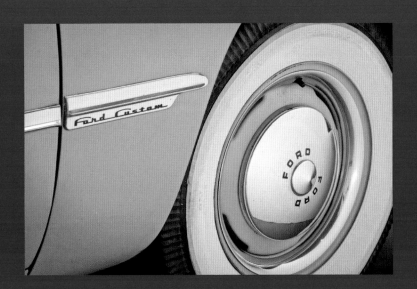

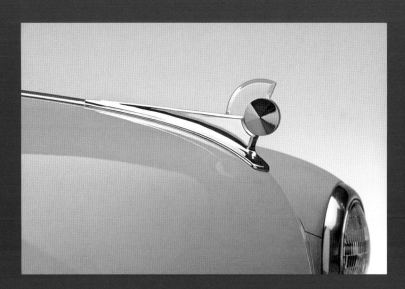

1956 FORD THUNDERBIRD CONVERTIBLE

To customers, the Thunderbird was a personal luxury car that combined sporty power and agility with the civilized appointments of a prestige model. To Ford, the Thunderbird was a "halo car" that attracted customers to showrooms. Unlike Chevrolet's similarly conceived Corvette, Ford stylists made sure that the Thunderbird's look reflected the company's less sophisticated models. The Thunderbird grew into a four-seater in 1958. It sold better but was never quite the same.

1962 FORD MUSTANG I ROADSTER

Ford unveiled the Mustang I at the 1962 U.S. Grand Prix. Purely a design exercise,
the car never went into production, but it generated excitement about Ford at car shows
and promotional events. The seats were integral with the body and not adjustable, so the
steering wheel and pedals moved instead. This led to further quirks. For instance,
the horn paddle switch was mounted on the center console.

1965 FORD MUSTANG CONVERTIBLE

Aware of the growing youth market, Lee Iacocca championed a sporty but inexpensive new car targeted at twenty- and thirty-somethings. To keep down costs, designers started with an existing Ford Falcon chassis and spiced it up with a stylish body and powerful engine. The car's exhaustive list of options meant that it could be almost anything to anyone, from a six-cylinder economy car to a powerful, factory-built hot rod. This Mustang bears serial number one.

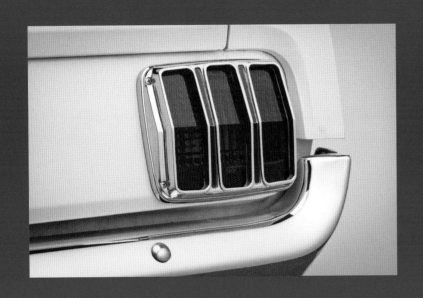

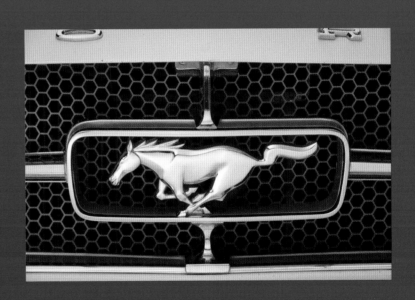

1967 FORD MARK IV RACE CAR

Dan Gurney and A. J. Foyt drove the Mark IV to victory at the 1967 24 Hours of Le
Mans. The win capped Ford's prodigious effort to establish itself as a performance brand
through racing, and it furthered the sport's evolution from a show of brute strength to a
scientific pursuit. The Mark IV's structure was made of aircraft-style, honeycombed
aluminum. Its engine sat between the driver and the rear axle, and its complex curves were
the result of careful wind-tunnel testing. The car remains in its original 1967 condition.

1981 FORD ESCORT GLX SEDAN

Following the Dodge Omni, Ford introduced its own European-inspired compact car
in 1980. In this case, however, "inspired" is too weak a word. Ford's European division
had been building Escorts since 1968. The U.S. version shared some of the European model's
components—though ultimately not as many as engineers had hoped. The Escort was
intended to be a "world car," built and sold around the globe. In keeping with this
universal ethos, it had a globe-shaped badge on the fender, and it conspicuously
lacked the Blue Oval logo on the grille.

1986 Ford Taurus LX Sedan

Given the Ford Taurus's quarter century of influence on auto design, it's hard to appreciate
just how different it looked when it arrived in late 1985. Family sedans were boxy and busy,
and yet here was a clean car without a single square edge. The user-friendly interior was
equally surprising with curving lines, sweptback instruments, and dimpled switches that
helped drivers adjust them by feel. The Taurus sold more than two hundred thousand units
in its first year, saved Ford from bankruptcy, and made aerodynamic styling mainstream.

1987 Ford Thunderbird Stock Car

Bill Elliot drove this stock car into the record books when he qualified for the 1987
Winston 500 at Talladega with a speed of 212.809 miles per hour. Yet the phrase "stock"
car was a misnomer by the 1980s. Elliot's racer *looked* like a Thunderbird but otherwise shared
nothing with the Thunderbirds on dealers' lots. In addition, NASCAR's growing popularity
had attracted new sponsors to the sport, including some—like Coors Brewing Company—
whose business had nothing to do with cars.

1991 FORD EXPLORER SPORT UTILITY VEHICLE

Prior to the Explorer, sport utility vehicles (SUVs) appealed to a niche market. (Think north woods campers or western cattle ranchers.) By softening the ride and smartening the interior, Ford turned the SUV into a viable substitute for the family car. The timing couldn't have been better, as gas was cheap and minivans were increasingly passé.

2009 FORD FOCUS ELECTRIC PROMOTIONAL VEHICLE

This is one of two custom electric Ford Focus automobiles built for *The Jay Leno Show.*
Leno's celebrity guests drove the cars around an obstacle course, trying to best one another's
times. The unusual campaign provided advanced publicity for the production electric Focus
introduced in 2012. It also furthered Ford's efforts to "green" the company through cars
with increased fuel efficiency and alternative power sources.

GM
Power Electronics
System 110
A Product of
Delco Propulsion Systems
Manufactured by Delco Electronics

1997 General Motors EV1 Electric Coupe

General Motors introduced its first all-electric car, the EV1, in 1996. Not ready to sell
the semi-experimental vehicle outright, GM leased it to the public. The drivers were loyal,
but the company concluded that the EV1 could never be profitable. GM canceled the leases
and destroyed most of the cars. Some suggested there was a sinister conspiracy between
the carmaker and oil companies; in reality, the EV1's limited range and two-person
capacity simply made it impractical.

1903 Holsman Runabout

Holsman's runabout was a primitive vehicle even by 1903 standards. Manila ropes transferred power to the drive wheels, a hand lever operated the brake, and the high wheels featured hard-rubber tires. But the basic design appealed to farmers, both for its mechanical simplicity and its ability to travel rough roads. Customers and roads soon got more sophisticated, but the Holsman did not. The company entered receivership in 1910.

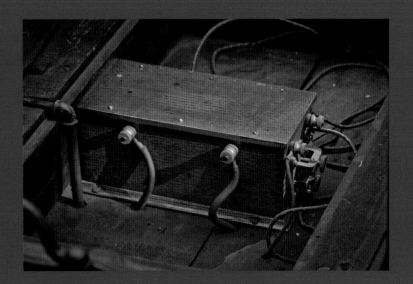

1989 HONDA ACCORD DX SEDAN

By 1975, Japan produced 70 percent of the foreign automobiles sold in America. When
the Big Three and the UAW called for higher import tariffs, Japanese firms shifted some
production to the United States. Honda opened its first American auto factory in 1982,
and Nissan, Toyota, and Mitsubishi followed suit. The line between "domestic" and
"import" blurred, and in 1989, the American-built Honda Accord became the
first Japanese marque to be the best-selling car in the United States.

1949 KAISER TRAVELER SEDAN

Smaller carmakers lacked the Big Three's resources, but their hunger produced inspired designs. Kaiser introduced an early crossover with its Traveler sedan. Drivers accessed the rear via a unique hatchback/tailgate combination. The back seat folded down for additional cargo room, and heavy-duty springs and shocks supported hefty loads. In addition, the spare tire sat out of the way against the left rear passenger door, which was welded shut.

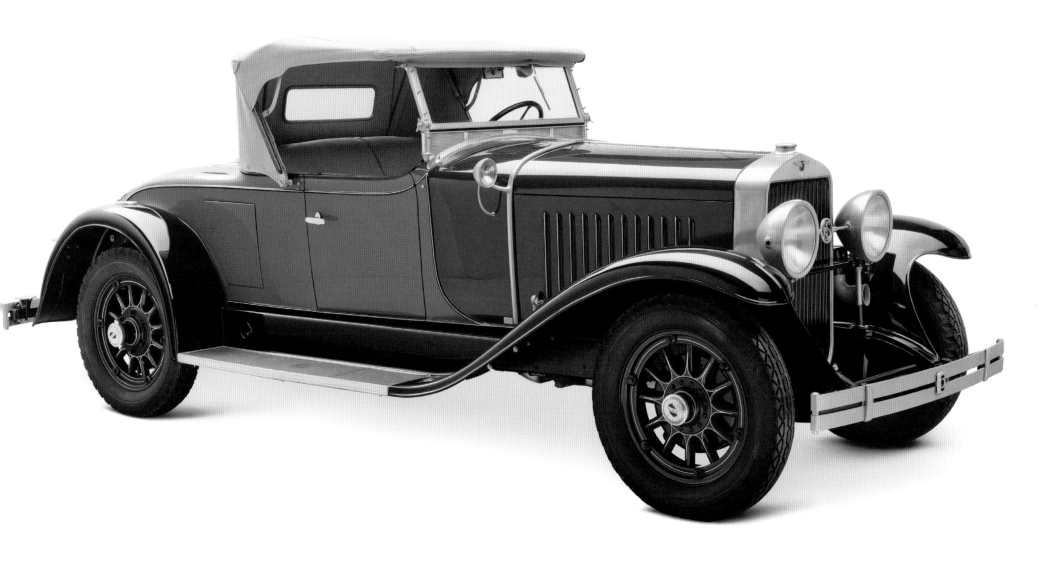

1927 LaSalle Roadster

Prior to the elegant mass-produced LaSalle, graceful styling was exclusive to high-end custom makes. General Motors introduced LaSalle in 1926 as a less expensive companion for Cadillac. Harley Earl came on board to design and launched a thirty-two-year career that produced some of America's most celebrated cars.

1937 LaSalle Coupe

When the Depression bit into sales, LaSalle struggled. The marque took a big hit to
its status when GM replaced the Cadillac-engineered V-8 with an Oldsmobile inline-8 in
the 1934–1936 models. When Packard's mid-priced One-Twenty further eroded sales,
LaSalle returned to Cadillac form in 1937, complete with the V-8. It wasn't enough
to save the brand, and LaSalle disappeared in 1940.

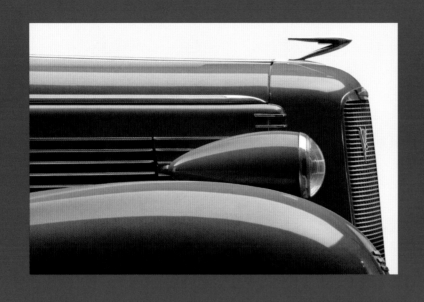

1936 LINCOLN ZEPHYR SEDAN

The Zephyr served as a lower-priced companion car to Lincoln proper. Yet less expensive did not mean inferior. The streamlined Zephyr was strikingly modern. The headlights blended into the fenders, the hood was hinged at the rear rather than the center, the windshield leaned back at a rakish angle, and the monocoque construction yielded a low body with merely vestigial running boards.

1939 LINCOLN PRESIDENTIAL LIMOUSINE

Franklin Roosevelt's 1939 Lincoln was the first car significantly altered for presidential use and the first to take hold in the public consciousness. Nicknamed the "Sunshine Special," the car was a perfect fit for a president whose unfailing cheer carried the nation through depression and war. Special storage compartments, wider running boards, and rear footboards distinguished the car from standard Lincolns. Armor plating and bulletproof glass were added soon after Pearl Harbor. President Truman retired the limo in 1950.

1950 LINCOLN PRESIDENTIAL LIMOUSINE

This 1950 Lincoln convertible joined the White House fleet in the waning months
of Harry Truman's administration. President Eisenhower had the car fitted with a removable
"bubbletop" that kept passengers visible even in poor weather. In addition to the president
himself, the limousine carried dignitaries like Queen Elizabeth II, Nikita Khrushchev,
and Charles de Gaulle. The car served through most of President Johnson's
administration before being retired to The Henry Ford in 1967.

1961 LINCOLN CONTINENTAL PRESIDENTIAL LIMOUSINE

President John F. Kennedy was assassinated in this car on November 22, 1963. In that instant, America's postwar calm was shattered and the turbulent 1960s began. The car as Kennedy knew it was fitted with footboards and transparent, removable roof panels. After the assassination, armor plating, bullet-resistant glass, and a permanent roof made the limo a true armored vehicle. The updated car served presidents Johnson, Nixon, Ford, and Carter before coming to The Henry Ford in 1978.

1972 LINCOLN CONTINENTAL PRESIDENTIAL LIMOUSINE

The replacement for the 1961 Lincoln limousine was a significant step in the evolution of presidential transport. Unlike previous vehicles modified for White House use, this 1972 Lincoln was custom built and armored from the start. Although it also served presidents Nixon, Ford, Carter, and George H. W. Bush, the car is most closely associated with Ronald Reagan, who found shelter inside it during the attempt on his life on March 30, 1981.

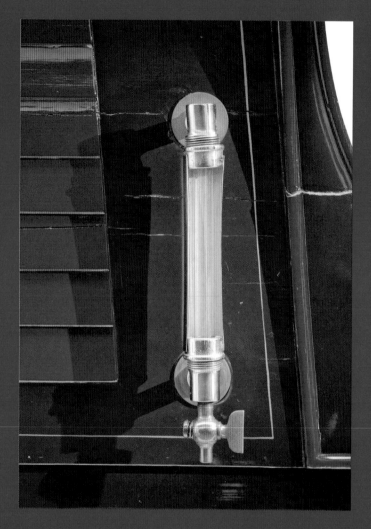

1899 LOCOMOBILE RUNABOUT

There was little in Locomobile's inexpensive steam cars to suggest that the company
would soon produce some of the finest luxury automobiles on the market. The 1899 model
had tiller steering, a chain drive, and a tube frame similar to a bicycle's. Quality improved
dramatically when Locomobile switched over to high-end gasoline cars in 1904.

1906 LOCOMOBILE "OLD 16" RACE CAR

In 1908, "Old 16" became the first American car to win the Vanderbilt Cup, the
first signature auto race in the United States. The Vanderbilt drew entrants from home and
abroad, and French marques dominated the first three races. Driver George Robertson's
victory in "Old 16" was about more than trophies and glory. It was proof that American
cars were every bit equal to their European counterparts. Never restored, "Old 16"
wears the same paint it carried across the finish line during its historic victory.

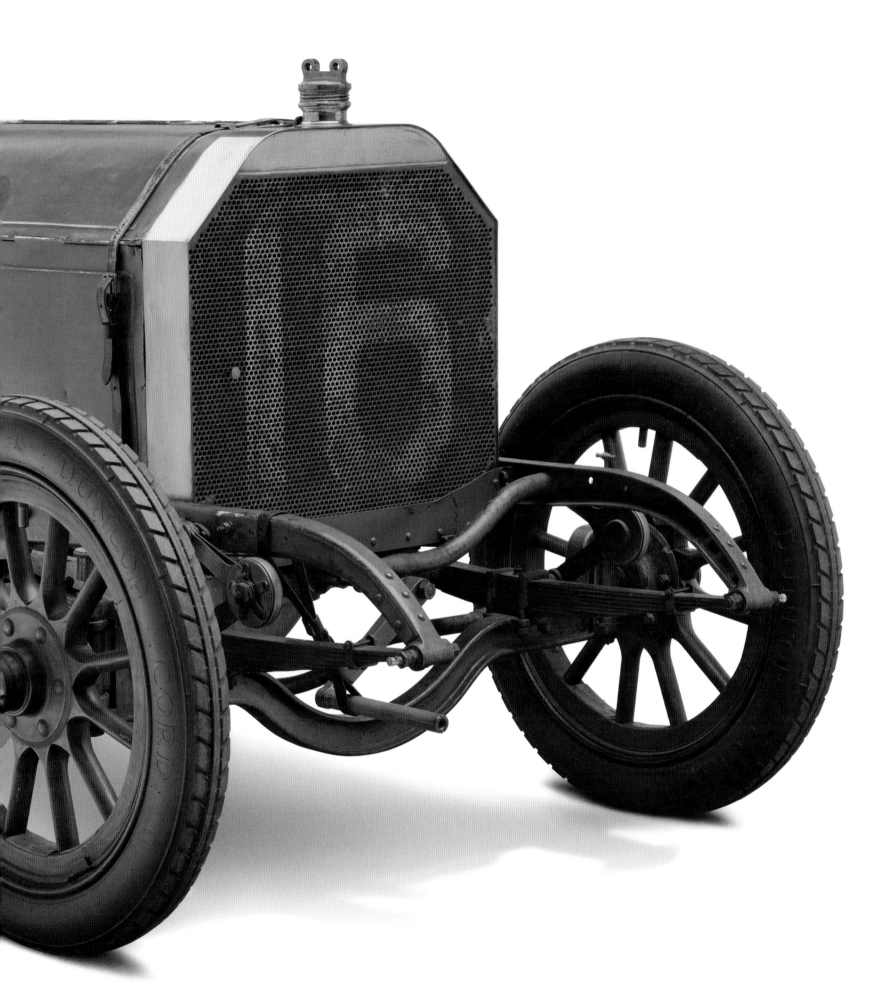

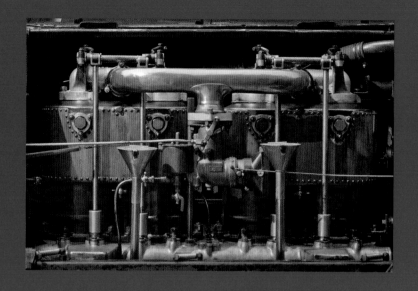

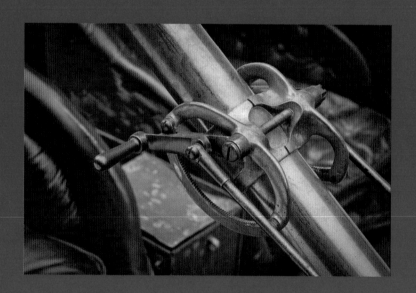

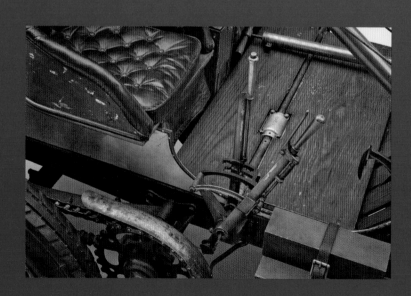

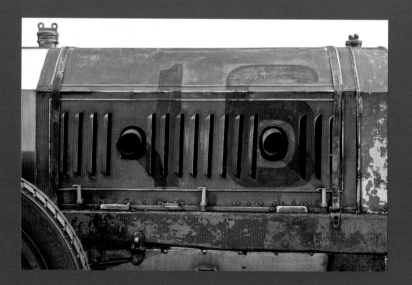

1965 LOTUS-FORD RACE CAR

Scotsman Jim Clark gave Ford's Total Performance racing program a major victory
at the 1965 Indianapolis 500. His car also changed the face of Indy racing. Clark's Formula
One–inspired racer combined a lightweight monocoque Lotus chassis with a powerful
rear-mounted Ford V-8. It was the antithesis of the heavy, front-engine roadsters
prevalent at Indy since World War II. Future entrants imitated the design, and the
most American of races acquired a decidedly European look.

1984 MARCH 84C-COSWORTH RACE CAR

The Indianapolis 500 may be the quintessential American race, but cars from the
British firm March Engineering dominated the event in the mid-1980s. This car, driven by
1983 winner Tom Sneva, posted a record qualifying speed of 210.029 miles per hour for 1984
but failed to finish the actual race due to a broken suspension. The car illustrates a sophisticated
understanding of the aerodynamics of racing. The front and rear wings push the vehicle
down, and ground effect tunnels create low pressure, further pulling it to the track.

1949 MERCURY CUSTOMIZED CONVERTIBLE

Customizing a car allowed an owner to put a unique stamp on what was otherwise a
mass-produced product. Postwar prosperity expanded the customization hobby, and with
their low lines and stunning curves, Mercury's 1949–1951 cars became the preferred canvas
for customizers' art. Tops were chopped, bodies were lowered, and sparkling metallic
paint jobs were added, turning personal transportation into personal statements.

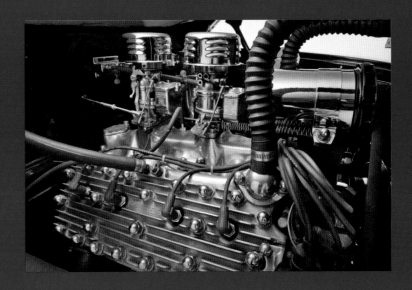

1968 MERCURY COUGAR COUPE

Mercury's Cougar brought flair to the pony car. The first Cougars drew heavily from
Mustang's look and mechanics but added a dash of European style. The corporate cousins
went their separate ways after the 1973 oil crisis. Mustang became a fuel-efficient
subcompact while Cougar moved into the personal luxury market. No longer simply
the "Mustang with class," the Cougar became the "junior Thunderbird."

1960 MESKOWSKI RACE CAR

Indy's brick and asphalt was racing's best-known track, but dirt tracks were the heart
and soul of American Championship racing until pavement became the rule in 1970.
Wally Meskowski's open-wheel racer was typical of the dirt-track era with a four-cylinder
Offenhauser engine, a two-speed transmission, and an aluminum body in a shape that had
remained largely the same since the 1930s. A. J. Foyt won the first of his record-setting
sixty-seven American Championship victories in this car.

1935 MILLER-FORD RACE CAR

Harry Miller's designs dominated American racing prior to World War II. His cars
combined technical innovation with exquisite craftsmanship. The 1935 Miller-Fords were
the first front-wheel-drive, four-wheel independent-suspension cars to race in the Indianapolis
500. Unfortunately, they were rushed into production without sufficient time for testing.
Excessive heat on the steering gear boxes, resulting from a design flaw, prevented all
of the Miller-Fords from finishing the race. This particular car did not qualify.

1950 NASH RAMBLER CONVERTIBLE

George Mason, CEO of Nash-Kelvinator, guessed that postwar suburban families would
want smaller second cars, and he introduced the compact Rambler in 1950. It was a winning
bet. Not only did Mason's gamble give Nash a niche market ignored by the Big Three, it
also helped the company—which later became part of American Motors—survive
until 1987, long after the other independents had vanished.

1903 OLDSMOBILE CURVED DASH RUNABOUT

The endearing Curved Dash Olds foreshadowed a shift in how cars were built and sold.
This was no fancy toy for the rich but a simple automobile within reach of middle-class
Americans. Production climbed from 425 units in 1901, to four thousand in 1903, to
six thousand in 1905. Soon after, the company shifted to larger cars, and the last
Curved Dash model left the plant in 1907.

1918 OVERLAND MODEL 90 B TOURING CAR

Charles Minshall and Claude E. Cox founded Overland in 1903. Minshall abandoned
the as-yet-unprofitable enterprise in 1905, and Cox left two years later when auto dealer
John North Willys bought the company and began to remake it. Willys's efforts paid off.
The Overland was America's second-best selling car from 1912 to 1918. It cost more
than the top-selling Model T, but it offered a sliding gear transmission,
wheel-mounted brakes, and a more comfortable ride.

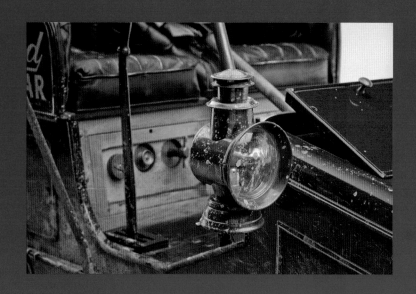

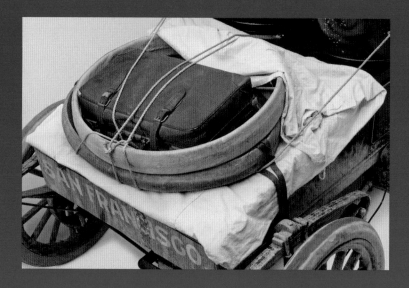

1903 PACKARD MODEL F RUNABOUT

In 1903, Tom Fetch and Marius Krarup drove this Packard Model F, nicknamed
"Old Pacific," from San Francisco to New York in sixty-one days. Theirs was only the
second transcontinental auto trip, and it was a significant feat at a time when roads were
still poor or nonexistent. But this technical achievement was mixed with old-fashioned
marketing: Packard provided gas and supplies along the way and then
profited handsomely from the trek's publicity.

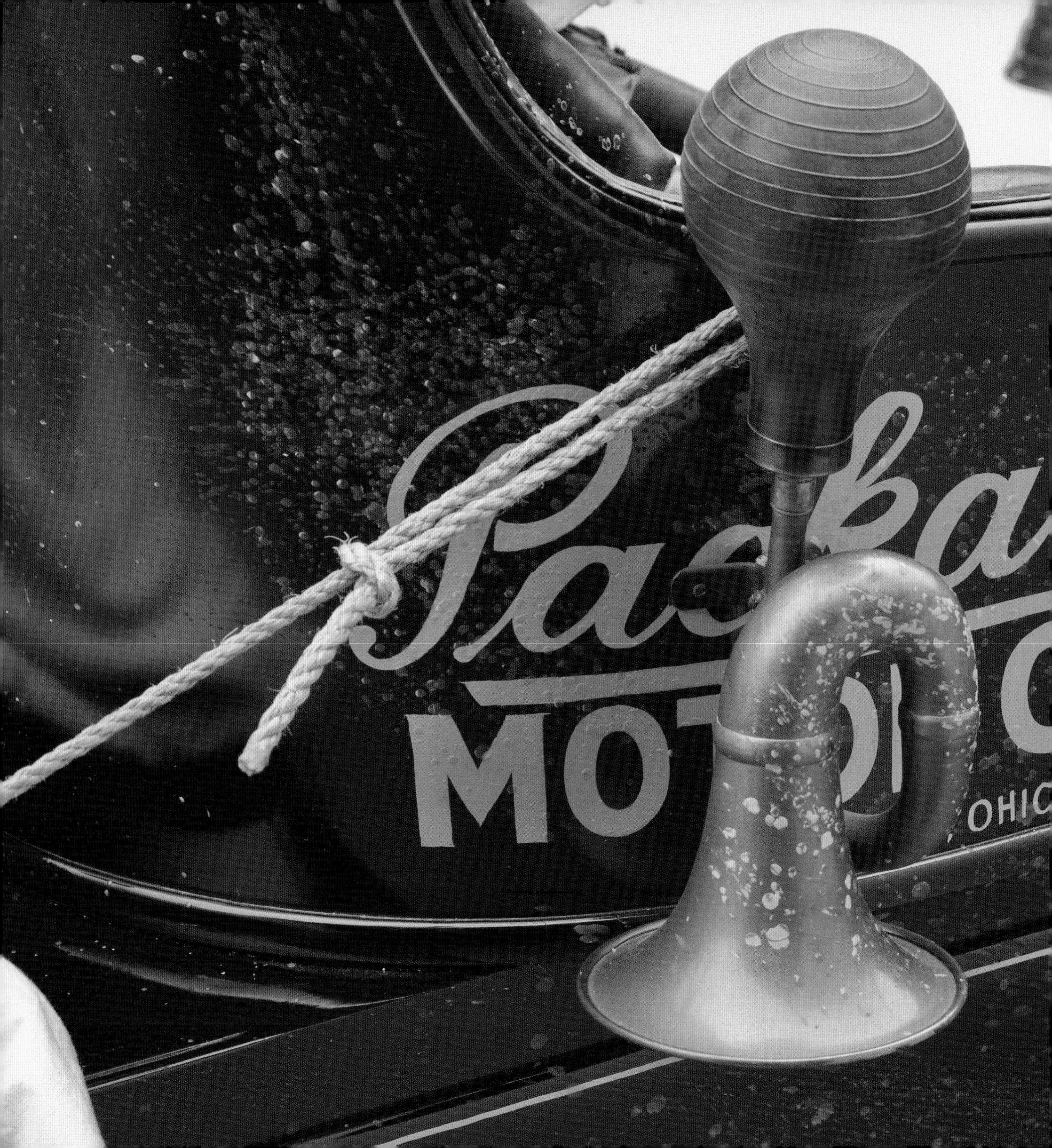

1904 PACKARD MODEL L TOURING CAR

Packard's earliest models, with steering wheels and "H" gearshift patterns, were fairly advanced, but the 1904 cars marked a significant shift from horseless carriage to true automobile. That year's offerings boasted four-cylinder engines and the "shouldered" radiator frames that became a company trademark. The change coincided with Packard's move to Detroit from its birthplace in Warren, Ohio.

1950 PLYMOUTH DELUXE SUBURBAN STATION WAGON

As its name suggests, the station wagon evolved from the horse-drawn hacks that carried travelers and their luggage between the railroad depot and hotel. Custom coach builders produced the earliest auto wagons by fitting specialized wooden bodies onto existing chassis. Carmakers started selling factory-built wagons in 1924, but the Depression soon affected sales. Custom builders that survived were finished off when Chrysler introduced the first steel-bodied wagon in 1949, and Ford and GM quickly followed suit.

1984 PLYMOUTH VOYAGER MINIVAN

Chrysler's renaissance under Lee Iacocca flourished with the minivan, which reimagined
the family car. The idea of a smaller van was not new, but Chrysler built its version on
a front-wheel-drive K-car platform. The transmission arrangement made the vehicle
roomier and allowed it to sit closer to the ground. The lower ride made it drive more
like a car and helped it fit in the family garage to boot.

1965 PONTIAC TEMPEST LeMANS GTO HARDTOP

Racing purists cried foul when Pontiac appropriated "GTO" from Ferrari, but no one
questioned the car's performance. The GTO accessories package turned the ho-hum Tempest
into a race-ready monster that swallowed a quarter mile in 14.8 seconds—and did so at
a price within reach of young drivers. The quintessential "halo car," the GTO cast
a glow of performance over the Pontiac line and launched the muscle car era.

1912 RAMBLER KNICKERBOCKER LIMOUSINE

Thomas B. Jeffery made the leap from building bicycles to automobiles in 1897. Five years
later, he moved his firm from Chicago to Kenosha, Wisconsin, to focus exclusively on cars,
but he kept the brand name Rambler. The 1912 limousine featured rich leather and mahogany
as well as a right-hand drive. The Rambler name vanished in 1914 only to reappear in
the 1950s, long after the Jeffrey Company had evolved into Nash Motors in 1916.

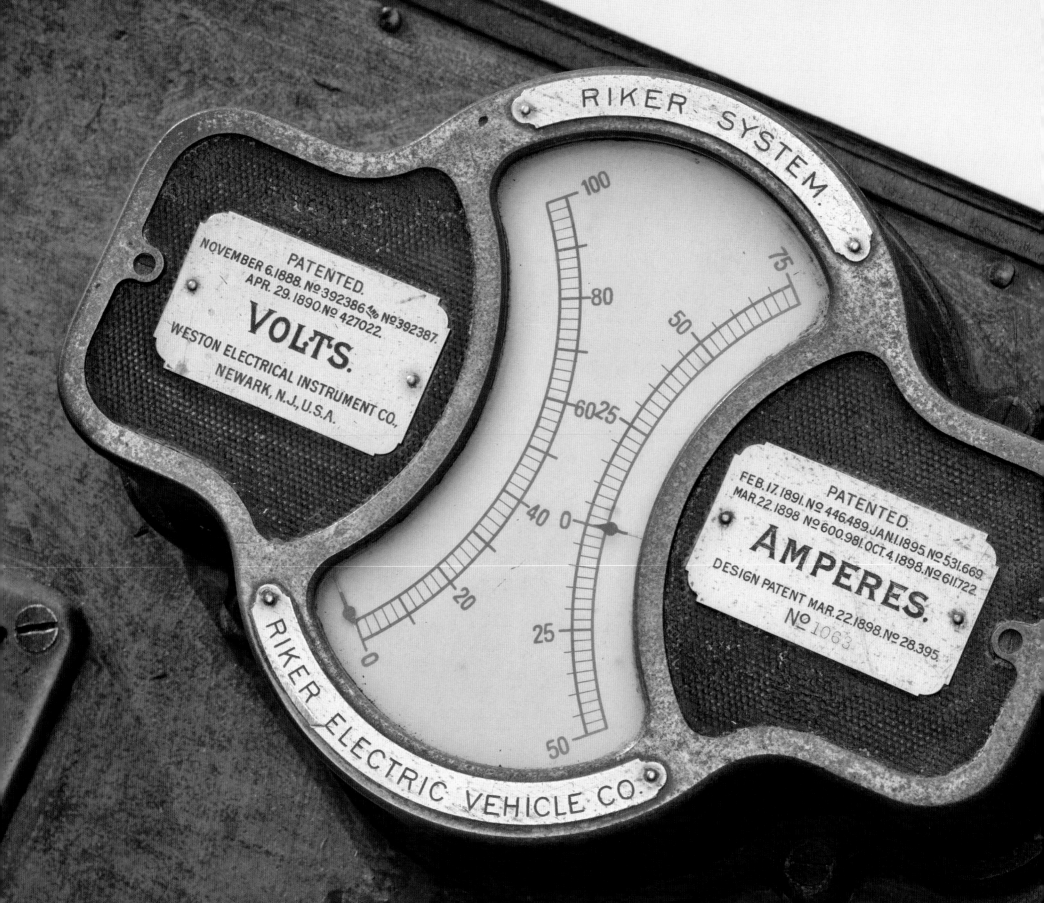

1896 RIKER ELECTRIC TRICYCLE

One year after building this electric tricycle for personal use, Andrew Lawrence Riker
began producing commercial electric vehicles. He soon tired of day-to-day business demands,
however, and turned to racing. Coming to believe that the future lay in gasoline power,
Riker sold his electric firm and joined Locomobile as chief engineer in 1900. He went
on to become the first president of the Society of Automotive Engineers.

1865 ROPER STEAM CARRIAGE

This is the oldest surviving American automobile. Sylvester Roper's steam carriages weren't the first self-propelled vehicles on U.S. roads, but W. W. Austen, Roper's canny promoter, ensured they would be the first to receive widespread notice. Roper carriages toured with circuses and were advertised as "the greatest mechanical exhibition in the world." Despite the publicity, Roper never attempted commercial production.

1913 SCRIPPS-BOOTH ROCKET CYCLECAR PROTOTYPE

For a few years, low-cost cyclecars appealed to consumers with tight budgets. The flimsy contraptions earned a reputation for poor quality which, combined with the Model T's declining price, hastened their demise. This prototype Rocket—named for the fuel tank protruding at the front—put the driver's controls in the rear seat. The four hundred or so production units had the driver's controls up front.

"JB·ROCKET" CYCLECARS·DETROIT·

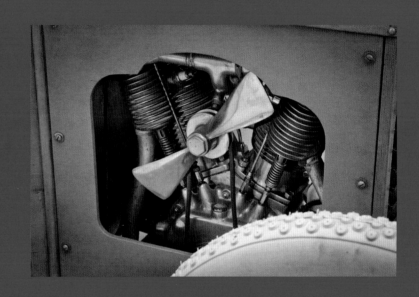

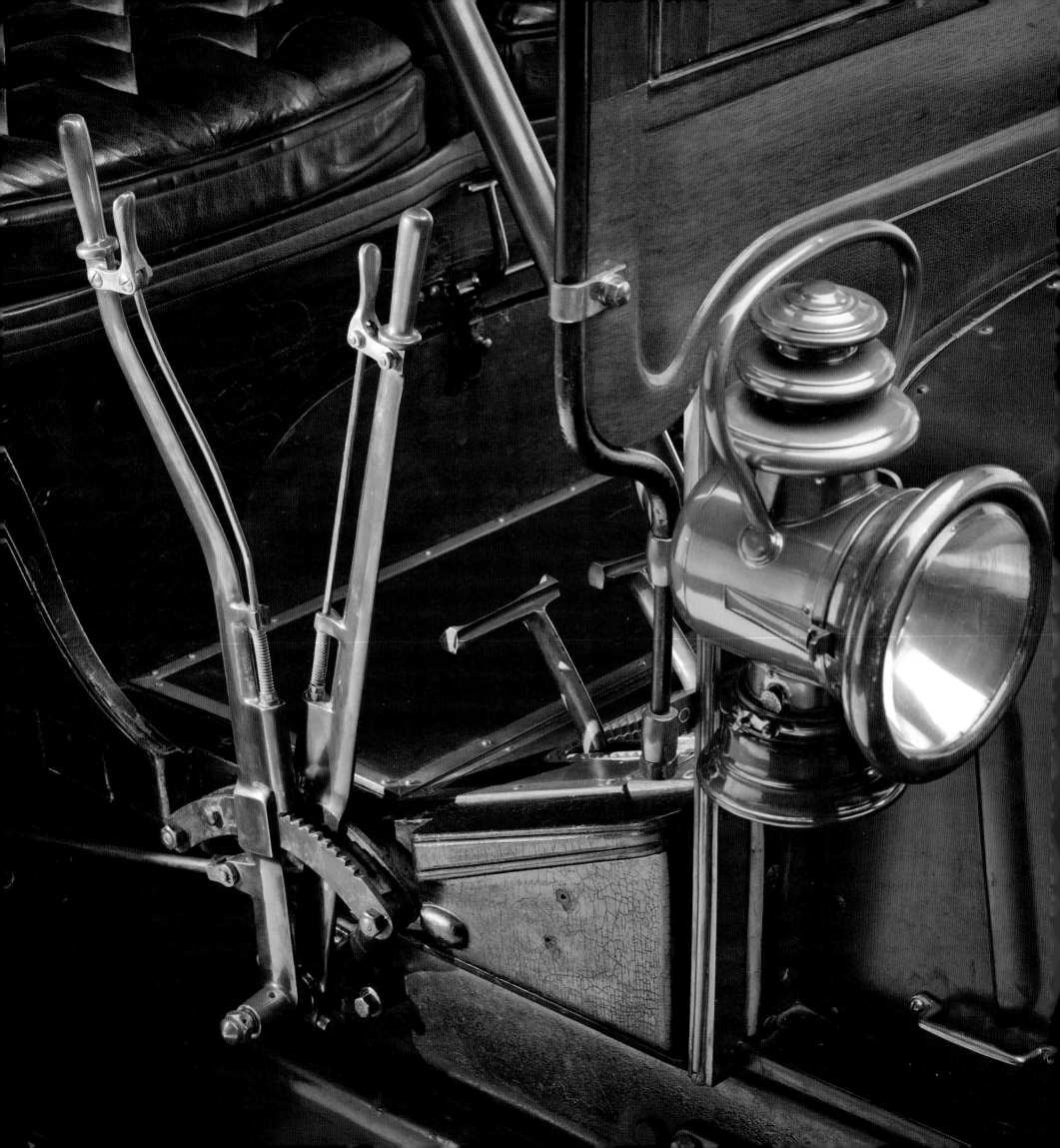

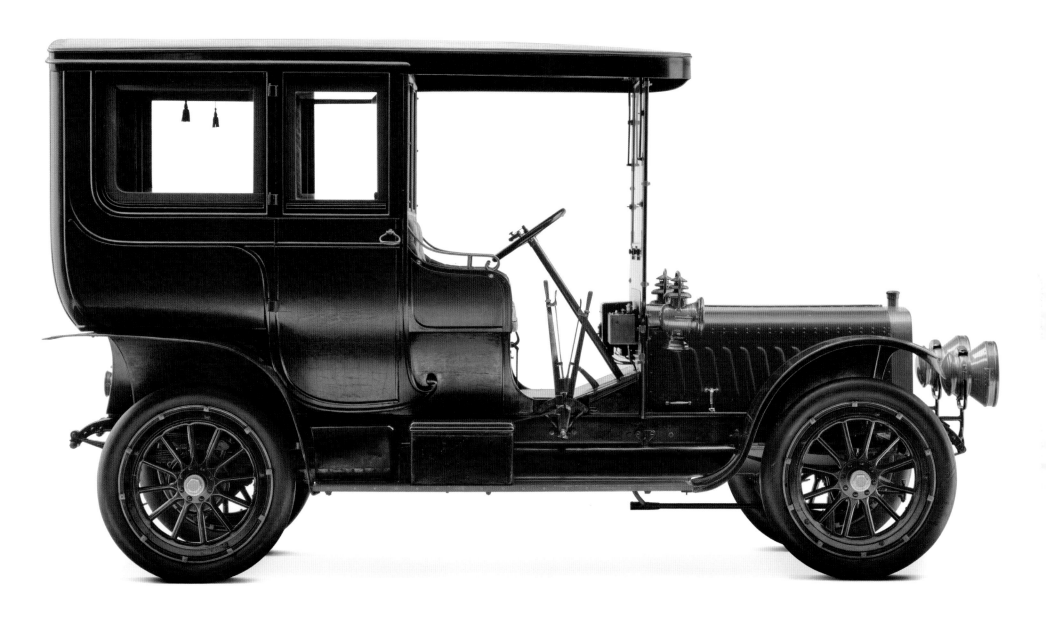

1908 STEVENS-DURYEA MODEL U LIMOUSINE

After severing business ties with his brother Charles, J. Frank Duryea teamed with
the J. Stevens Arms and Tool Company to form Stevens-Duryea in 1901. While the company
marketed some smaller autos, big touring cars and limousines were its bread and butter.
Money got tight, however, and Frank Duryea sold his stake in 1915. The company
carried on through receivership and a succession of new owners before closing in 1927.

1951 STUDEBAKER CHAMPION STARLIGHT COUPE

Studebaker enjoyed a reputation as a style leader. It introduced the first all-new postwar
car in 1946 and employed talented designers like Raymond Lowey, Virgil Exner, and Bob
Bourke. The "bullet-nose" cars of 1950 and 1951 were surely the company's most
distinctive efforts. Despite—or perhaps because of—their unconventional appearance,
the cars sold well and gave Studebaker its best production and sales years.

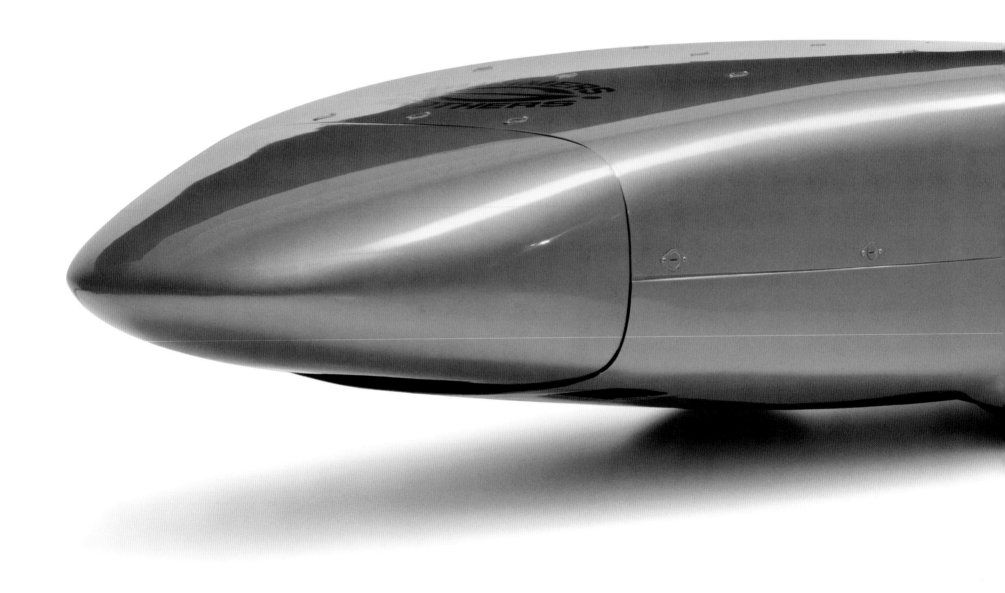

1965 GOLDENROD LAND SPEED RACE CAR

Jet-powered vehicles dominated land speed records in the 1960s, but Bob and Bill Summers's
wheel-driven Goldenrod claimed its share of glory. The brothers squeezed four Chrysler
Hemi engines into a sleek aluminum body just forty-eight inches wide but thirty-two feet
long. Bob Summers drove Goldenrod to 409.277 miles per hour on November 12, 1965.
There was no prize money, but the brothers had the satisfaction of setting
a land speed record that stood for twenty-six years.

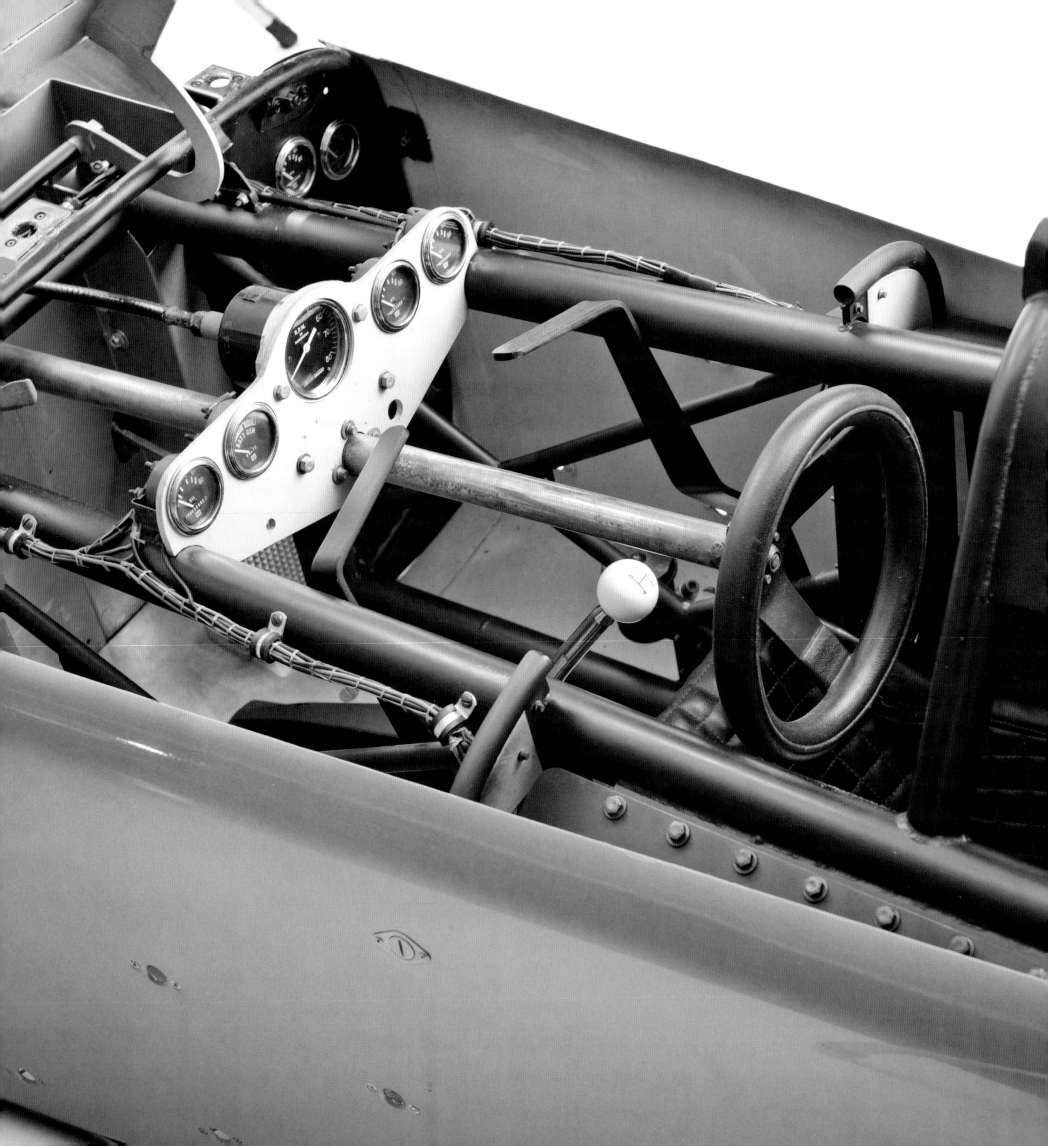

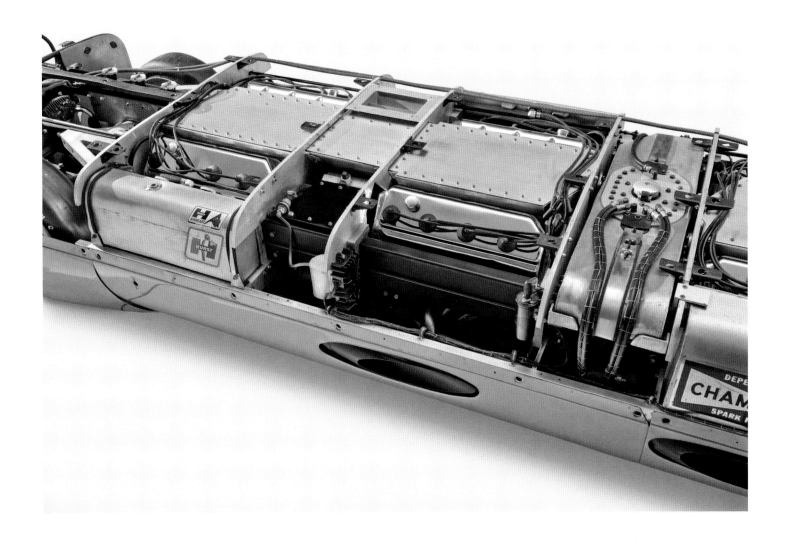

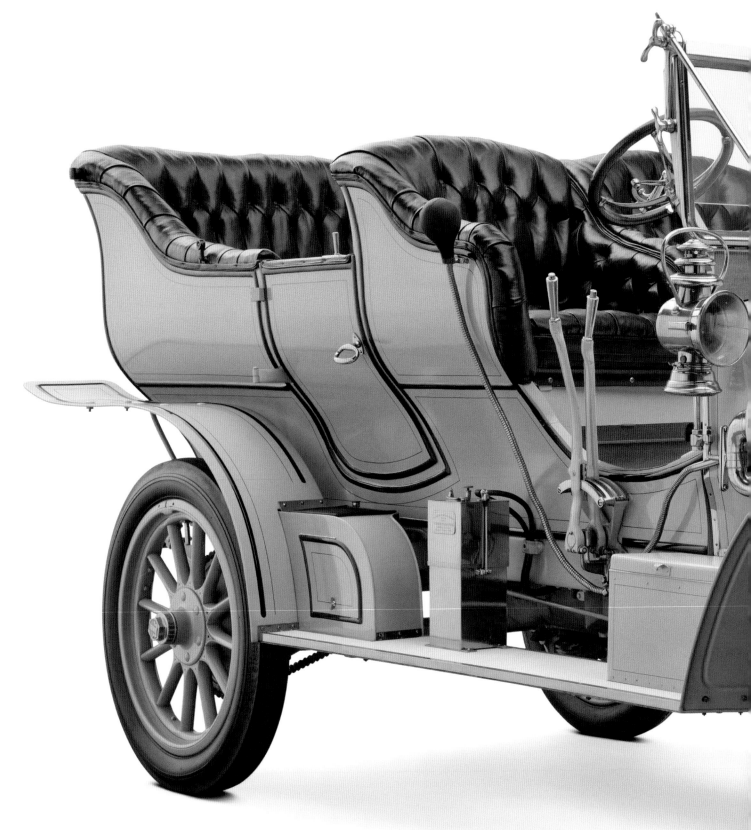

1906 THOMAS FLYER TOURING CAR

Erwin Ross Thomas built bicycles before transitioning to automobiles in 1900. Though
Thomas's first efforts drew heavily on cycle design, he soon produced quality automobiles
with sliding-gear transmissions and roller bearings. The company's zenith came in 1908
when a Thomas Flyer won the grueling New York to Paris Race. After Thomas
left the firm in 1911, sales slumped. The company folded in 1918.

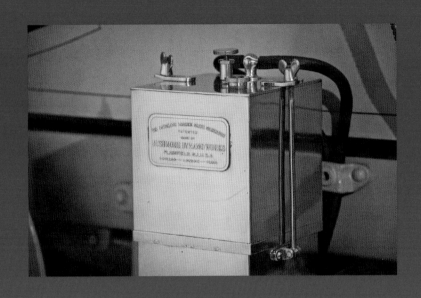
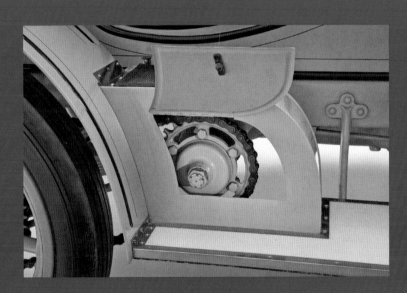

1966 TOYOTA CORONA SEDAN

Introduced for the 1965 model year, the Corona was the first Japanese car designed
specifically for the American market. It was smaller than the Big Three's compacts, which
grew as the 1960s wore on, but could cruise comfortably along the interstate at seventy
miles per hour. The Corona was a quality car that kept improving—as did Japanese
automakers' fortunes in the United States.

2002 TOYOTA PRIUS SEDAN

At the turn of the twenty-first century, with gas prices rising and air quality falling,
some automakers marketed hybrid gasoline-electric cars. Toyota introduced the Prius
in Japan in 1997 and worldwide in 2000. The electric motor did all the work until the
batteries ran low or higher speeds were required. The Prius's $20,000 price tag was
steep for a compact, but tax credits offset some of the cost, and drivers got
a little environmental peace of mind in the deal, too.

1948 TUCKER 48 SEDAN

Postwar Americans were hungry for new cars, which created a golden opportunity for new
makers. Preston Tucker wooed buyers with an unconventional automobile that featured a
rear-mounted engine, doors that cut into the roof, and a distinctive center headlight that turned
with the front wheels. Yet Tucker's financing methods were equally novel, and he was soon
charged with fraud. Though cleared by a jury, Tucker closed his company after producing
just fifty-one cars. The Tucker 48's dramatic look and promising features, as well as Preston
Tucker's independent challenge to the Big Three, instilled the car with a lasting mystique.

1949 VOLKSWAGEN SEDAN

It's hard to imagine a tougher sell in the postwar United States: a plain, scrawny car that was championed by Adolph Hitler. But the Volkswagen was a brilliant alternative to big, flashy American cars. The vehicle's basic appointments kept costs low, the rear-mounted engine maximized space, and the streamlined body boosted fuel economy. Germany's "people's car" echoed the Model T in spirit and ultimately outsold it with over twenty-one million units.

1959 Volkswagen Westfalia Camper

Volkswagen's Type 2 was innovative, but its larger legacy is its place in popular culture—or,
counterculture—as the hippie's transport of choice. The Type 2 shared the sedan's rear-engine
platform and endearing looks. Passenger versions had removable rear seats, while commercial
variants left the rear open for cargo. Volkswagen contracted with Westfalia to build campers
with folding seats, iceboxes, and water storage tanks. These well-equipped recreational
vehicles were decidedly more appropriate for parents and children than flower children.

1907 White Model G Steam Touring Car

White Motor Company, an offshoot of a sewing machine manufacturer, produced its first steam car in 1900 and hit peak annual sales of 1,534 in 1906. The company's hallmarks were the engine's placement under the hood—unusual for a steam car—and the lithe, "White curve" arch on the hood. White added gasoline cars to its line in 1910 before shifting exclusively to commercial vehicle production in 1918. The firm remained in business until 1980.

1933 WILLYS DRAG RACER

George Montgomery's 1933 Willys was a crowd favorite at drag strips in California and the Midwest. The Class AA/Gas Supercharged cars were popular with race fans because they looked like street vehicles—even if they weren't actually street legal. Montgomery drove his 1933 Willys to six National Hot Rod Association class championships in the 1950s and 1960s, constantly modifying the car to stay competitive. "Ohio George" proved that he could more than hold his own against the California hot rodders who dominated the sport.

1943 WILLYS-OVERLAND JEEP RUNABOUT

With World War II on the horizon, the army put out a call for a lightweight,
four-cylinder, four-wheel-drive vehicle. American Bantam provided the winning design,
and Willys-Overland and Ford produced most of the 650,000 Jeeps built for military use.
Postwar civilian versions were modest sellers, but they set the stage for the wildly
popular sport utility vehicles of the 1980s and 1990s.

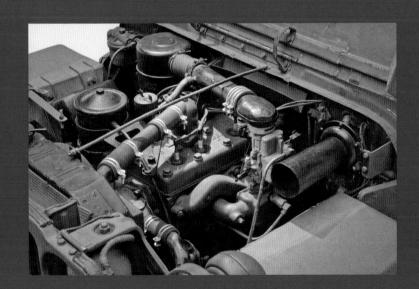
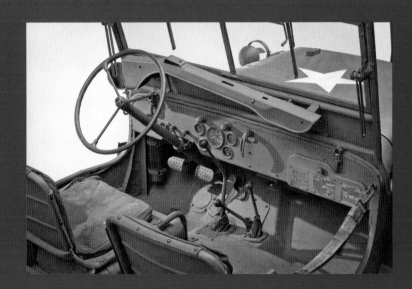

1916 WOODS DUAL-POWER HYBRID COUPE

Depending on one's point of view, the Woods Dual-Power was an idea too far ahead
of its time or one that came too late. Having built electric cars since 1899, Woods watched
that market evaporate in the 1910s. To survive, it introduced a car with an electric motor
that was used up to fifteen miles per hour and a gasoline engine for speeds up to thirty-five.
The idea was clever, but it couldn't save the company, which folded in 1918.

THE SPECIFICATIONS

1951 BEATTY BELLY TANK LAKESTER LAND SPEED RACE CAR

PAGES: 34–35

MAKER
Tom Beatty, Sun Valley, California

ENGINE
Oldsmobile V-8, overhead valves, supercharged, 260 cubic inches

TRANSMISSION
4-speed automatic

HORSEPOWER: 400
HEIGHT: 45 inches
WHEELBASE: 110 inches

WIDTH: 69 inches
OVERALL LENGTH: 177 inches
WEIGHT: 2,165 pounds

COMPETITION HISTORY:
Fastest car in its class at Bonneville National Speed Trials in 1951, 1952, 1955, 1959, and 1962.

1915 BREWSTER TOWN LANDAULET

PAGE: 36

MAKER
Brewster & Company, New York, New York

ENGINE
Inline-4, sleeve valves, 276 cubic inches

TRANSMISSION
3-speed manual

HORSEPOWER: 55
HEIGHT: 82.5 inches
WHEELBASE: 125 inches

WIDTH: 66 inches
OVERALL LENGTH: 173 inches
WEIGHT: 4,150 pounds

PRICE: $7,600

1960 BUCK & THOMPSON SLINGSHOT DRAGSTER

PAGE: 37

MAKER
Sam Buck and Bob Thompson, Lockport, Illinois

ENGINE
Ford V-8, L-head valves, 320 cubic inches

TRANSMISSION
1948 Ford 3-speed manual using only 2nd and 3rd gears

HORSEPOWER: 220 (estimate)
HEIGHT: 50 inches
WHEELBASE: 96 inches

WIDTH: 60 inches
OVERALL LENGTH: 148 inches
WEIGHT: 1,210 pounds

COMPETITION HISTORY:
Winner of Class D Dragster, World Series of Drag Racing, Cordova, Illinois, 1961; Winner of Class D Dragster, U.S. Fuel & Gas Championships, Bakersfield, California, 1962.

1931 BUGATTI TYPE 41 ROYALE CONVERTIBLE

PAGES: 38–41

MAKER/ BODY MAKER
Ettore Bugatti, Molsheim, France/ Weinberger, Munich, Germany

ENGINE
Inline-8, overhead cam, 779 cubic inches

TRANSMISSION
3-speed manual

HORSEPOWER: 300
HEIGHT: 62.5 inches
WHEELBASE: 169 inches

WIDTH: 82.5 inches
OVERALL LENGTH: 233 inches
WEIGHT: 7,035 pounds

PRICE: $43,000

1963 BUICK RIVIERA COUPE	1959 CADILLAC ELDORADO BIARRITZ CONVERTIBLE	1981 CHECKER MARATHON TAXICAB	1915 CHEVROLET ROYAL MAIL ROADSTER

PAGES: 42-43

PAGES: 44-47

PAGES: 48-49

PAGES: 50-51

MAKER
General Motors Corporation,
Detroit, Michigan

MAKER
General Motors Corporation,
Detroit, Michigan

MAKER
Checker Motors Corporation,
Kalamazoo, Michigan

MAKER
Chevrolet Motor Company,
Flint, Michigan

ENGINE
V-8, overhead valves, 401 cubic
inches

ENGINE
V-8, overhead valves, 390 cubic
inches

ENGINE
V-6, overhead valves, 229 cubic
inches

ENGINE
Inline-4, overhead valves, 171
cubic inches

TRANSMISSION
3-speed automatic

TRANSMISSION
4-speed automatic

TRANSMISSION
3-speed automatic

TRANSMISSION
3-speed manual, nonsynchromesh

HORSEPOWER: 325 @ 4,400 rpm
HEIGHT: 53.5 inches
WHEELBASE: 117 inches

HORSEPOWER: 345 @ 4,800 rpm
HEIGHT: 54.5 inches
WHEELBASE: 130 inches

HORSEPOWER: 110 @ 4,200 rpm
HEIGHT: 63 inches
WHEELBASE: 120 inches

HORSEPOWER: 24
HEIGHT: 77 inches
WHEELBASE: 106 inches

WIDTH: 77 inches
OVERALL LENGTH: 208 inches
WEIGHT: 3,998 pounds

WIDTH: 81 inches
OVERALL LENGTH: 225 inches
WEIGHT: 5,060 pounds

WIDTH: 76 inches
OVERALL LENGTH: 205 inches
WEIGHT: 3,680 pounds

WIDTH: 66.5 inches
OVERALL LENGTH: 146 inches
WEIGHT: 2,000 pounds

PRICE: $4,333

PRICE: $7,401

PRICE: $9,632

PRICE: $750

1955 Chevrolet Corvette Roadster	1955 Chevrolet Bel Air Hardtop	1956 Chevrolet Bel Air Convertible	1960 Chevrolet Corvair Sedan

PAGES: 52–55	PAGES: 56–59	PAGES: 60–61	PAGE: 62

MAKER General Motors Corporation, Detroit, Michigan	**MAKER** General Motors Corporation, Detroit, Michigan	**MAKER** General Motors Corporation, Detroit, Michigan	**MAKER** General Motors Corporation, Detroit, Michigan
ENGINE V-8, overhead valves, 265 cubic inches	**ENGINE** V-8, overhead valves, 265 cubic inches	**ENGINE** V-8, overhead valves, 265 cubic inches	**ENGINE** Horizontally opposed 6, overhead valves, 140 cubic inches
TRANSMISSION 2-speed automatic	**TRANSMISSION** 3-speed manual	**TRANSMISSION** 2-speed automatic	**TRANSMISSION** 2-speed automatic

HORSEPOWER: 195 @ 5,000 rpm HEIGHT: 48 inches WHEELBASE: 102 inches	HORSEPOWER: 162 @ 4,400 rpm HEIGHT: 60.5 inches WHEELBASE: 115 inches	HORSEPOWER: 225 @ 4,600 rpm HEIGHT: 59 inches WHEELBASE: 115 inches	HORSEPOWER: 80 @ 4,400 rpm HEIGHT: 51.5 inches WHEELBASE: 108 inches
WIDTH: 72 inches OVERALL LENGTH: 167 inches WEIGHT: 2,705 pounds	WIDTH: 74 inches OVERALL LENGTH: 195.5 inches WEIGHT: 3,165 pounds	WIDTH: 74 inches OVERALL LENGTH: 197.5 inches WEIGHT: 3,320 pounds	WIDTH: 66.5 inches OVERALL LENGTH: 180 inches WEIGHT: 2,305 pounds
PRICE: $2,934	PRICE: $2,166	PRICE: $2,538	PRICE: $2,038

1924 CHRYSLER TOURING CAR

PAGE: 63

MAKER
Maxwell Motor Corporation, Highland Park, Michigan

ENGINE
Inline-6, L-head valves, 201 cubic inches

TRANSMISSION
3-speed manual

HORSEPOWER: 68 @ 3,000 rpm
HEIGHT: 69 inches
WHEELBASE: 113 inches

WIDTH: 68 inches
OVERALL LENGTH: 160 inches
WEIGHT: 2,785 pounds

PRICE: $1,395

1956 CHRYSLER 300-B STOCK CAR

PAGES: 64–67

MAKER
Chrysler Corporation, Highland Park, Michigan

ENGINE
V-8, overhead valves, 352 cubic inches

TRANSMISSION
3-speed manual

HORSEPOWER: 355
HEIGHT: 54.5 inches
WHEELBASE: 126 inches

WIDTH: 79 inches
OVERALL LENGTH: 220.5 inches
WEIGHT: 4,145 pounds

COMPETITION HISTORY:
It's impossible to say which races this car won in 1956, because the team didn't keep track of wins by particular cars. Overall, the Kiekhaefer Chryslers won 22 of 41 races in 1956.

1963 CHRYSLER TURBINE SEDAN

PAGES: 68–71

MAKER
Chrysler Corporation, Highland Park, Michigan

ENGINE
Regenerative gas turbine

TRANSMISSION
3-speed automatic

HORSEPOWER: 130 @ 3,600 rpm, output shaft
HEIGHT: 53.5 inches
WHEELBASE: 110 inches

WIDTH: 73 inches
OVERALL LENGTH: 201.5 inches
WEIGHT: 3,900 pounds

PRICE: N/A

1973 CHRYSLER NEWPORT SEDAN

PAGES: 72–73

MAKER
Chrysler Corporation, Highland Park, Michigan

ENGINE
V-8, overhead valves, 400 cubic inches

TRANSMISSION
3-speed automatic

HORSEPOWER: 185 @ 3,600 rpm
HEIGHT: 56 inches
WHEELBASE: 124 inches

WIDTH: 79.5 inches
OVERALL LENGTH: 230 inches
WEIGHT: 4,200 pounds

PRICE: $4,693

1901 COLUMBIA VICTORIA

PAGES: 74–75

MAKER
Electric Vehicle Company, Hartford, Connecticut

MOTOR
80-volt DC

HORSEPOWER: 6 @ 1,620 rpm
HEIGHT: 84 inches
WHEELBASE: 86 inches

WIDTH: 64.5 inches
OVERALL LENGTH: 133.5 inches
WEIGHT: 3,250 pounds

PRICE: $3,500

1956 CONTINENTAL MARK II SEDAN

PAGES: 76–77

MAKER
Ford Motor Company, Dearborn, Michigan

ENGINE
V-8, overhead valves, 368 cubic inches

TRANSMISSION
3-speed automatic

HORSEPOWER: 300 @ 4,800 rpm
HEIGHT: 56 inches
WHEELBASE: 126 inches

WIDTH: 77.5 inches
OVERALL LENGTH: 218.5 inches
WEIGHT: 4,825 pounds

PRICE: $9,966

1980 COMUTA-CAR ELECTRIC RUNABOUT

PAGES: 78-79

MAKER
Commuter Vehicles, Inc., Sebring, Florida

ENGINE
DC, lead-acid batteries, 48 volts

RANGE
40 miles

HORSEPOWER: 5
HEIGHT: 58 inches
WHEELBASE: 63 inches

WIDTH: 55 inches
OVERALL LENGTH: 95 inches
WEIGHT: 1,300 pounds

PRICE: $5,000

1937 CORD 812 CONVERTIBLE

PAGES: 80-83

MAKER
Auburn Automobile Company, Auburn, Indiana

ENGINE
V-8, L-head valves, 289 cubic inches

TRANSMISSION
4-speed manual

HORSEPOWER: 125 @ 3,500 rpm
HEIGHT: 58 inches
WHEELBASE: 125 inches

WIDTH: 73 inches
OVERALL LENGTH: 195.5 inches
WEIGHT: 3,863 pounds

PRICE: $2,645

<table>
<tr>
<td>

1957 CORNELL-LIBERTY
CONCEPT SAFETY CAR

</td>
<td>

1951 CROSLEY
HOTSHOT ROADSTER

</td>
<td>

1957 DE SOTO
FIREFLITE HARDTOP

</td>
<td>

1914 DETROIT ELECTRIC
MODEL 47 BROUGHAM

</td>
</tr>
</table>

MAKER/ FUNDER Cornell Aeronautical Laboratory, Buffalo, New York/Liberty Mutual Insurance Company, Boston, Massachusetts	**MAKER** Crosley Motors, Inc., Cincinnati, Ohio	**MAKER** Chrysler Corporation, Highland Park, Michigan	**MAKER** Anderson Electric Car Company, Detroit, Michigan
ENGINE V-8, overhead valves, 272 cubic inches	**ENGINE** Inline-4, overhead cam, 44 cubic inches	**ENGINE** V-8, overhead valves, 341 cubic inches	**MOTOR** DC
TRANSMISSION N/A	**TRANSMISSION** 3-speed manual	**TRANSMISSION** 3-speed automatic	**BATTERIES** 54 cells, 108 volts

HORSEPOWER: N/A HEIGHT: 63 inches WHEELBASE: 116 inches	HORSEPOWER: 26.5 @ 5,400 rpm HEIGHT: 50 inches WHEELBASE: 85 inches	HORSEPOWER: 295 @ 4,600 rpm HEIGHT: 55 inches WHEELBASE: 126 inches	HORSEPOWER: Unknown HEIGHT: 84.5 inches WHEELBASE: 100 inches
WIDTH: 75 inches OVERALL LENGTH: 207 inches WEIGHT: N/A	WIDTH: 48 inches OVERALL LENGTH: 148.5 inches WEIGHT: 1,184 pounds	WIDTH: 78 inches OVERALL LENGTH: 218 inches WEIGHT: 4,125 pounds	WIDTH: 72 inches OVERALL LENGTH: 142.5 inches WEIGHT: 3,636 pounds
PRICE: N/A	PRICE: $924	PRICE: $3,671	PRICE: $3,730

1978 Dodge Omni Sedan

PAGE: 94

MAKER
Chrysler Corporation, Highland Park, Michigan

ENGINE
Inline-4, overhead valves, 105 cubic inches

TRANSMISSION
3-speed automatic

HORSEPOWER: 75 @ 5,600 rpm
HEIGHT: 53.5 inches
WHEELBASE: 99 inches

WIDTH: 66 inches
OVERALL LENGTH: 165 inches
WEIGHT: 2,145 pounds

PRICE: $3,976

1998 Dodge Ram Quad Cab Pickup Truck

PAGE: 95

MAKER
Chrysler Corporation, Auburn Hills, Michigan

ENGINE
V-8, overhead valves, 360 cubic inches

TRANSMISSION
4-speed automatic

HORSEPOWER: 245 @ 4,000 rpm
HEIGHT: 72 inches
WHEELBASE: 139 inches

WIDTH: 79 inches
OVERALL LENGTH: 225 inches
WEIGHT: 4,788 pounds

PRICE: $20,410

1931 Duesenberg Model J Convertible Victoria

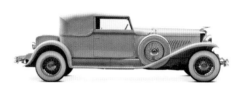

PAGES: 96–99

MAKER/ BODY MAKER
Duesenberg, Inc., Indianapolis, Indiana/Rollston, New York, New York

ENGINE
Inline-8, double overhead cams, 420 cubic inches

TRANSMISSION
3-speed manual, nonsynchromesh

HORSEPOWER: 265 @ 4,200 rpm
HEIGHT: 68 inches
WHEELBASE: 153.5 inches

WIDTH: 72 inches
OVERALL LENGTH: 211.5 inches
WEIGHT: 4,900 pounds

PRICE: $13,000 (estimate)

1896 Duryea Runabout

PAGES: 100–101

MAKER
Duryea Motor Wagon Company, Springfield, Massachusetts

ENGINE
Inline-2, F-head valves, 138 cubic inches

TRANSMISSION
3-speed manual

HORSEPOWER: 6
HEIGHT: 59 inches
WHEELBASE: 60 inches

WIDTH: 56 inches
OVERALL LENGTH: 94 inches
WEIGHT: 700 pounds

PRICE: $1,500 (estimate)

1899 DURYEA TRAP

PAGE: 102

MAKER
Duryea Manufacturing Company,
Peoria, Illinois

ENGINE
Inline-3, 215 cubic inches

TRANSMISSION
2-speed manual

HORSEPOWER: 6
HEIGHT: 51 inches
WHEELBASE: 66 inches

WIDTH: 62 inches
OVERALL LENGTH: 102 inches
WEIGHT: 700 pounds

PRICE: $1,200

2010 EDISON2 CONCEPT CAR

PAGE: 103

MAKER
Edison2, Charlottesville, Virginia

ENGINE
1-cylinder, double overhead cam,
turbocharged, 15 cubic inches

TRANSMISSION
6-speed manual

HORSEPOWER: 40
HEIGHT: 53 inches
WHEELBASE: 100 inches

WIDTH: 79 inches
OVERALL LENGTH: 167 inches
WEIGHT: 830 pounds

PRICE: N/A

1958 EDSEL CITATION HARDTOP

PAGES: 104–107

MAKER
Ford Motor Company, Dearborn,
Michigan

ENGINE
V-8, overhead valves, 410 cubic
inches

TRANSMISSION
3-speed automatic

HORSEPOWER: 345 @ 4,600 rpm
HEIGHT: 57 inches
WHEELBASE: 124 inches

WIDTH: 80 inches
OVERALL LENGTH: 219 inches
WEIGHT: 4,136 pounds

PRICE: $3,500

1924 ESSEX COACH SEDAN

PAGES: 108–109

MAKER
Hudson Motor Car Company,
Detroit, Michigan

ENGINE
Inline-6, L-head valves, 130 cubic
inches

TRANSMISSION
3-speed manual

HORSEPOWER: 35
HEIGHT: 71.5 inches
WHEELBASE: 110.5 inches

WIDTH: 64 inches
OVERALL LENGTH: 156.5 inches
WEIGHT: 2,305 pounds

PRICE: $975

1896 QUADRICYCLE RUNABOUT	1901 FORD "SWEEPSTAKES" RACE CAR	1902 FORD "999" RACE CAR	1903 FORD MODEL A RUNABOUT

PAGES: 110–111	PAGES: 112–113	PAGES: 114–115	PAGE: 116

MAKER Henry Ford, Detroit, Michigan, with David Bell, James Bishop, George Cato, and Edward Huff **ENGINE** Inline-2, F-head valves, 59 cubic inches **TRANSMISSION** 2-speed manual	**MAKER** Henry Ford, Oliver Barthel, and Edward Huff, Detroit, Michigan **ENGINE** Horizontally opposed 2, atmospheric intake valves and mechanical exhaust valves, 539 cubic inches **TRANSMISSION** 2-speed manual	**MAKER** Henry Ford, Tom Cooper, and Edward Huff, Detroit, Michigan **ENGINE** Inline-4, atmospheric intake valves and mechanical exhaust valves, 1,156 cubic inches **TRANSMISSION** None, in-and-out clutch	**MAKER** Ford Motor Company, Detroit, Michigan **ENGINE** Horizontally opposed 2, L-head valves, 100 cubic inches **TRANSMISSION** 2-speed manual

HORSEPOWER: 4 @ 500 rpm (estimate) HEIGHT: 45 inches WHEELBASE: 49 inches WIDTH: 45.5 inches OVERALL LENGTH: 78.5 inches WEIGHT: 500 pounds PRICE: N/A	HORSEPOWER: 26 @ 900 rpm HEIGHT: 57 inches WHEELBASE: 96 inches WIDTH: 62 inches OVERALL LENGTH: 133 inches WEIGHT: 2,430 pounds COMPETITION HISTORY: Winner of 10-mile race against Alexander Winton, Grosse Pointe, Michigan, 1901. Driver: Henry Ford.	HORSEPOWER: 80 @ 700 rpm HEIGHT: 50 inches WHEELBASE: 117 inches WIDTH: 55 inches OVERALL LENGTH: 145 inches WEIGHT: 2,730 pounds COMPETITION HISTORY: Winner of five-mile race against Alexander Winton and two other drivers at Grosse Pointe, Michigan, 1902. Driver: Barney Oldfield.	HORSEPOWER: 8 HEIGHT: 57 inches WHEELBASE: 72 inches WIDTH: 65 inches OVERALL LENGTH: 103 inches WEIGHT: 1,250 pounds PRICE: $850

1905 FORD MODEL B TOURING CAR	1906 FORD MODEL N RUNABOUT	1908 FORD MODEL S ROADSTER	1909 FORD MODEL T TOURING CAR

PAGE: 117	PAGES: 118–119	PAGES: 120–121	PAGES: 122–125

MAKER	**MAKER**	**MAKER**	**MAKER**
Ford Motor Company, Detroit, Michigan	Ford Motor Company, Detroit, Michigan	Ford Motor Company, Detroit, Michigan	Ford Motor Company, Detroit, Michigan
ENGINE	**ENGINE**	**ENGINE**	**ENGINE**
Inline-4, L-head valves, 284 cubic inches	Inline-4, L-head valves, 149 cubic inches	Inline-4, L-head valves, 149 cubic inches	Inline-4, L-head valves, 177 cubic inches
TRANSMISSION	**TRANSMISSION**	**TRANSMISSION**	**TRANSMISSION**
2-speed manual	2-speed manual	2-speed manual	2-speed manual

HORSEPOWER: 24	HORSEPOWER: 15	HORSEPOWER: 15	HORSEPOWER: 22 @ 1,600 rpm
HEIGHT: 77.5 inches	HEIGHT: 64 inches (with top down)	HEIGHT: 61.5 inches	HEIGHT: 83 inches
WHEELBASE: 92 inches	WHEELBASE: 84 inches	WHEELBASE: 84 inches	WHEELBASE: 100 inches
WIDTH: 69.5 inches		WIDTH: 67 inches	WIDTH: 68 inches
OVERALL LENGTH: 103 inches	WIDTH: 63.5 inches	OVERALL LENGTH: 119 inches	OVERALL LENGTH: 134.5 inches
WEIGHT: 1,700 pounds	OVERALL LENGTH: 115 inches	WEIGHT: 1,100 pounds	WEIGHT: 1,200 pounds
	WEIGHT: 1,050 pounds		
PRICE: $2,000		PRICE: $750	PRICE: $850
	PRICE: $500		

1914 FORD
MODEL T TOURING CAR

PAGES: 126–127

MAKER
Ford Motor Company, Detroit, Michigan

ENGINE
Inline-4, L-head valves, 177 cubic inches

TRANSMISSION
2-speed manual

HORSEPOWER: 20 @ 1,600 rpm
HEIGHT: 76 inches
WHEELBASE: 100 inches

WIDTH: 65 inches
OVERALL LENGTH: 134.5 inches
WEIGHT: 1,200 pounds

PRICE: $550

1919 FORD MODEL T SEDAN

PAGES: 128–129

MAKER
Ford Motor Company, Dearborn, Michigan

ENGINE
Inline-4, L-head valves, 177 cubic inches

TRANSMISSION
2-speed manual

HORSEPOWER: 20 @ 1,600 rpm
HEIGHT: 73 inches
WHEELBASE: 100 inches

WIDTH: 67.5 inches
OVERALL LENGTH: 134.5 inches
WEIGHT: 1,875 pounds

PRICE: $875

1930 FORD
MODEL A TOURING CAR

PAGES: 130–131

MAKER
Ford Motor Company, Dearborn, Michigan

ENGINE
Inline-4, L-head valves, 201 cubic inches

TRANSMISSION
3-speed manual

HORSEPOWER: 40 @ 2,200
HEIGHT: 72 inches
WHEELBASE: 103.5 inches

WIDTH: 64 inches
OVERALL LENGTH: 149 inches
WEIGHT: 2,285 pounds

PRICE: $645

1932 FORD ROADSTER

PAGES: 132–135

MAKER
Dick Smith, Phoenix, Arizona, using a Ford body and chassis, Chrysler engine, Packard transmission, and Studebaker, Chevrolet, Ford, and Dodge parts

ENGINE
Chrysler V-8, overhead valves, 331 cubic inches

TRANSMISSION
3-speed manual

HORSEPOWER: 180 @ 4,000 rpm
HEIGHT: 56 inches
WHEELBASE: 106 inches

WIDTH: 65.5 inches
OVERALL LENGTH: 147 inches
WEIGHT: 2,459 pounds

PRICE: N/A

1932 FORD V-8 CABRIOLET	1939 FORD DELUXE CONVERTIBLE COUPE	1949 FORD TUDOR SEDAN	1956 FORD THUNDERBIRD CONVERTIBLE

PAGES: 136–139	PAGES: 140–141	PAGES: 142–143	PAGES: 144–147
MAKER Ford Motor Company, Dearborn, Michigan	**MAKER** Ford Motor Company, Dearborn, Michigan	**MAKER** Ford Motor Company, Dearborn, Michigan	**MAKER** Ford Motor Company, Dearborn, Michigan
ENGINE V-8, L-head valves, 221 cubic inches	**ENGINE** V-8, L-head valves, 221 cubic inches	**ENGINE** V-8, L-head valves, 239 cubic inches	**ENGINE** V-8, overhead valves, 312 cubic inches
TRANSMISSION 3-speed manual	**TRANSMISSION** 3-speed manual	**TRANSMISSION** 3-speed manual	**TRANSMISSION** 3-speed automatic
HORSEPOWER: 65 @ 3,400 rpm HEIGHT: 67 inches WHEELBASE: 106 inches	HORSEPOWER: 90 @ 3,800 rpm HEIGHT: 68.5 inches WHEELBASE: 112 inches	HORSEPOWER: 100 @ 3,600 rpm HEIGHT: 64.5 inches WHEELBASE: 114 inches	HORSEPOWER: 225 @ 4,600 rpm HEIGHT: 52 inches WHEELBASE: 102 inches
WIDTH: 79 inches OVERALL LENGTH: 165.5 inches WEIGHT: 2,398 pounds	WIDTH: 69.5 inches OVERALL LENGTH: 179.5 inches WEIGHT: 2,840 pounds	WIDTH: 73 inches OVERALL LENGTH: 197 inches WEIGHT: 2,988 pounds	WIDTH: 70.5 inches OVERALL LENGTH: 175.5 inches WEIGHT: 3,088 pounds
PRICE: $610	PRICE: $790	PRICE: $1,590	PRICE: $3,151

1962 FORD
MUSTANG I ROADSTER

PAGES: 148–151

MAKER
Ford Motor Company, Dearborn, Michigan

ENGINE
60-degree V-4, 91 cubic inches

TRANSMISSION
4-speed manual

HORSEPOWER: 109 @ 6,400 rpm
HEIGHT: 39.5 inches
WHEELBASE: 90 inches

WIDTH: 61 inches
OVERALL LENGTH: 154 inches
WEIGHT: 1,544 pounds

PRICE: N/A

1965 FORD
MUSTANG CONVERTIBLE

PAGES: 152–153

MAKER
Ford Motor Company, Dearborn, Michigan

ENGINE
V-8, overhead valves, 260 cubic inches

TRANSMISSION
3-speed automatic

HORSEPOWER: 164 @ 4,400 rpm
HEIGHT: 51 inches
WHEELBASE: 108 inches

WIDTH: 68 inches
OVERALL LENGTH: 182 inches
WEIGHT: 2,740 pounds

PRICE: $3,334

1967 FORD
MARK IV RACE CAR

PAGES: 154–155

MAKER
Ford Motor Company, Dearborn, Michigan

ENGINE
Ford V-8, overhead valves, 427 cubic inches

TRANSMISSION
4-speed manual

HORSEPOWER: 500 @ 5,000 rpm
HEIGHT: 38.5 inches
WHEELBASE: 70.5 inches

WIDTH: 95 inches
OVERALL LENGTH: 171 inches
WEIGHT: 2,205 pounds

COMPETITION HISTORY:
Appeared in only one race, the 1967 Le Mans 24-hour. It won, finishing 32 miles ahead of the second-place Ferrari, and set an average speed record of 135.48 mph.

1981 FORD
ESCORT GLX SEDAN

PAGE: 156

MAKER
Ford Motor Company, Dearborn, Michigan

ENGINE
Inline-4, overhead cam, 98 cubic inches

TRANSMISSION
4-speed manual

HORSEPOWER: 65 @ 5,600 rpm
HEIGHT: 53.5 inches
WHEELBASE: 94.5 inches

WIDTH: 66 inches
OVERALL LENGTH: 164 inches
WEIGHT: 2,029 pounds

PRICE: $6,577

1986 FORD TAURUS LX SEDAN	1987 FORD THUNDERBIRD STOCK CAR	1991 FORD EXPLORER SPORT UTILITY VEHICLE	2009 FORD FOCUS ELECTRIC PROMOTIONAL VEHICLE

PAGE: 157	PAGES: 158–159	PAGES: 160–161	PAGES: 162–163

MAKER
Ford Motor Company, Dearborn, Michigan

ENGINE
V-6, overhead valves, 182 cubic inches

TRANSMISSION
4-speed automatic

HORSEPOWER: 140 @ 4,000 rpm
HEIGHT: 54 inches
WHEELBASE: 106 inches

WIDTH: 71 inches
OVERALL LENGTH: 188 inches
WEIGHT: 2,863 pounds

PRICE: $15,022

MAKER
Ford Motor Company, Dearborn, Michigan

ENGINE
Ford V-8, overhead valves, 351 cubic inches

TRANSMISSION
4-speed manual

HORSEPOWER: 625
HEIGHT: 51 inches
WHEELBASE: 110 inches

WIDTH: 71 inches
OVERALL LENGTH: 197.5 inches
WEIGHT: 3,700 pounds

COMPETITION HISTORY:
Fastest qualifier for the 1987 Winston 500, Talladega, Alabama, at 212.809 mph. This remains NASCAR's fastest official lap ever. Won the 1987 Talladega 500, Talladega, Alabama.

MAKER
Ford Motor Company, Dearborn, Michigan

ENGINE
V-6, overhead valves, 244 cubic inches

TRANSMISSION
4-speed automatic, four-wheel drive

HORSEPOWER: 155 @ 3,800 rpm
HEIGHT: 67.5 inches
WHEELBASE: 112 inches

WIDTH: 70 inches
OVERALL LENGTH: 184.5 inches
WEIGHT: 4,015 pounds

PRICE: $19,275

MAKER
Ford Motor Company, Dearborn, Michigan

BASE CAR
2009 European-specification Ford Focus

MODIFICATIONS
Internal-combustion engine replaced by electric motor and batteries, suspension enhanced to improve handling

GREEN CAR CHALLENGE SETUP:
Roll bar and 5-point racing-harness seatbelt (since removed)

HEIGHT: 59 inches
WHEELBASE: 104 inches

WIDTH: 70 inches
OVERALL LENGTH: 165 inches
WEIGHT: 3,421 pounds

PRICE: N/A

1997 GENERAL MOTORS EV1 ELECTRIC COUPE	1903 HOLSMAN RUNABOUT	1989 HONDA ACCORD DX SEDAN	1949 KAISER TRAVELER SEDAN

PAGES: 164–165

PAGES: 166–167

PAGES: 168–169

PAGES: 170–173

MAKER
General Motors Corporation, Detroit, Michigan

MOTOR
3-phase inductive AC

BATTERIES
26 lead-acid, 312 volts

MAKER
Holsman Automobile Company, Chicago, Illinois

ENGINE
Horizontally opposed 2, T-head valves, 64 cubic inches

TRANSMISSION
2-speed manual

MAKER
American Honda Motor Company, Gardena, California

ENGINE
Inline-4, overhead cam, 119 cubic inches

TRANSMISSION
4-speed automatic

MAKER
Kaiser-Frazer Corporation, Willow Run, Michigan

ENGINE
Inline-6, L-head valves, 226 cubic inches

TRANSMISSION
3-speed manual

HORSEPOWER: 137 @ 7,000 rpm
HEIGHT: 50.5 inches
WHEELBASE: 99 inches

WIDTH: 69.5 inches
OVERALL LENGTH: 169.5 inches
WEIGHT: 2,790 pounds

LEASE PRICE: $399–$549 per month

HORSEPOWER: 5
HEIGHT: 63.5 inches
WHEELBASE: 60 inches

WIDTH: 64 inches
OVERALL LENGTH: 105.5 inches
WEIGHT: 650 pounds

PRICE: $675

HORSEPOWER: 98 @ 5,500 rpm
HEIGHT: 53.5 inches
WHEELBASE: 102.5 inches

WIDTH: 67.5 inches
OVERALL LENGTH: 180 inches
WEIGHT: 2,579 pounds

PRICE: $13,460

HORSEPOWER: 100 @ 3,600 rpm
HEIGHT: 64.5 inches
WHEELBASE: 123.5 inches

WIDTH: 73 inches
OVERALL LENGTH: 206.5 inches
WEIGHT: 3,456 pounds

PRICE: $2,088

1927 LaSalle Roadster	1937 LaSalle Coupe	1936 Lincoln Zephyr Sedan	1939 Lincoln Presidential Limousine

PAGES: 174–175

PAGES: 176–179

PAGES: 180–183

PAGES: 184–185

MAKER
General Motors Corporation, Detroit, Michigan

ENGINE
V-8, 303 cubic inches

TRANSMISSION
3-speed manual

HORSEPOWER: 75 @ 3,000 rpm
HEIGHT: 68 inches
WHEELBASE: 125 inches

WIDTH: 74 inches
OVERALL LENGTH: 185 inches
WEIGHT: 3,755 pounds

PRICE: $2,525

MAKER
General Motors Corporation, Detroit, Michigan

ENGINE
V-8, L-head valves, 322 cubic inches

TRANSMISSION
3-speed manual

HORSEPOWER: 125 @ 3,400 rpm
HEIGHT: 67 inches
WHEELBASE: 124 inches

WIDTH: 74 inches
OVERALL LENGTH: 201 inches
WEIGHT: 3,675 pounds

PRICE: $995

MAKER
Ford Motor Company, Dearborn, Michigan

ENGINE
V-12, L-head valves, 267 cubic inches

TRANSMISSION
3-speed manual, synchromesh on top 2 speeds

HORSEPOWER: 110 @ 3,900 rpm
HEIGHT: 68 inches
WHEELBASE: 122 inches

WIDTH: 71.5 inches
OVERALL LENGTH: 202.5 inches
WEIGHT: 3,349 pounds

PRICE: $1,320

MAKER
Ford Motor Company, Dearborn, Michigan, and Brunn & Company, Buffalo, New York

ENGINE
V-12, L-head valves, 414 cubic inches

TRANSMISSION
3-speed manual

HORSEPOWER: 150
HEIGHT: 73 inches
WHEELBASE: 161 inches

WIDTH: 76.5 inches
OVERALL LENGTH: 245 inches
WEIGHT: 9,300 pounds

PRICE: N/A

1950 LINCOLN PRESIDENTIAL LIMOUSINE

PAGES: 186–187

MAKER
Ford Motor Company, Dearborn, Michigan, and Dietrich Creative Industries, Grand Rapids, Michigan

ENGINE
V-8, L-head valves, 337 cubic inches

TRANSMISSION
4-speed automatic

HORSEPOWER: 152
HEIGHT: 65 inches
WHEELBASE: 145 inches

WIDTH: 80 inches
OVERALL LENGTH: 262 inches
WEIGHT: 6,500 pounds

PRICE: N/A

1961 LINCOLN CONTINENTAL PRESIDENTIAL LIMOUSINE

PAGES: 188–191

MAKER
Ford Motor Company, Dearborn, Michigan, and Hess & Eisenhardt Company, Cincinnati, Ohio

ENGINE
V-8, overhead valves, 430 cubic inches

TRANSMISSION
3-speed automatic

HORSEPOWER: 350
HEIGHT: 61 inches
WHEELBASE: 156 inches

WIDTH: 80 inches
OVERALL LENGTH: 252 inches
WEIGHT: 9,800 pounds

PRICE: N/A

1972 LINCOLN CONTINENTAL PRESIDENTIAL LIMOUSINE

PAGES: 192–193

MAKER
Ford Motor Company, Dearborn, Michigan

ENGINE
V-8, overhead valves, 460 cubic inches

TRANSMISSION
3-speed automatic

HORSEPOWER: 214
HEIGHT: 61 inches
WHEELBASE: 161 inches

WIDTH: 80 inches
OVERALL LENGTH: 259 inches
WEIGHT: 13,000 pounds

PRICE: N/A

1899 LOCOMOBILE RUNABOUT

PAGES: 194–195

MAKER
Locomobile Company of America, Watertown, Massachusetts

ENGINE
2-cylinder steam, double acting, 2.5" bore x 3.5" stroke

HORSEPOWER: 4 @ 150 psi
HEIGHT: 72 inches
WHEELBASE: 58 inches

WIDTH: 63 inches
OVERALL LENGTH: 114.5 inches
WEIGHT: 700 pounds

PRICE: $600

1906 LOCOMOBILE "OLD 16" RACE CAR	1965 LOTUS-FORD RACE CAR	1984 MARCH 84C-COSWORTH RACE CAR	1949 MERCURY CUSTOMIZED CONVERTIBLE

PAGES: 196–199

PAGES: 200–201

PAGES: 202–203

PAGES: 204–207

MAKER
Locomobile, Bridgeport, Connecticut

ENGINE
Locomobile inline-4, F-head valves, 990 cubic inches

TRANSMISSION
3-speed manual

MAKER
Lotus Cars, Cheshunt, England, and Ford Motor Company, Dearborn, Michigan

ENGINE
Ford V-8, double overhead cams, 256 cubic inches

TRANSMISSION
2-speed manual

MAKER
March Engineering, Bicester, England

ENGINE
Cosworth V-8, double overhead cams, turbocharged, 159 cubic inches

TRANSMISSION
5-speed manual

MAKER
Ford Motor Company, Dearborn, Michigan, and Barris Kustom Industries, North Hollywood, California

ENGINE
V-8, L-head valves, 276 cubic inches

TRANSMISSION
3-speed manual

HORSEPOWER: 120 @ 1,000 rpm
HEIGHT: 62 inches
WHEELBASE: 110 inches

WIDTH: 64 inches
OVERALL LENGTH: 163 inches
WEIGHT: 2,204 pounds

COMPETITION HISTORY:
Won the 1906 Elimination Race for American cars to qualify for the Vanderbilt Cup. Set the fastest lap during the 1906 Vanderbilt race. Won the 1908 Vanderbilt race and set the fastest lap.

HORSEPOWER: 495 @ 8,800 rpm
HEIGHT: 31 inches
WHEELBASE: 96 inches

WIDTH: 73 inches
OVERALL LENGTH: 156 inches
WEIGHT: 1,250 pounds

COMPETITION HISTORY:
Qualified second for the 1965 Indianapolis 500 and finished first, averaging 150.686 mph. Driver: Jim Clark.

HORSEPOWER: 740 @ 11,000 rpm
HEIGHT: 36 inches
WHEELBASE: 111 inches

WIDTH: 81 inches
OVERALL LENGTH: 180 inches
WEIGHT: 1,510 pounds

COMPETITION HISTORY:
Fastest qualifier, 1984 Indianapolis 500. Retired from the race while running second.

HORSEPOWER: 280
HEIGHT: 53.5 inches
WHEELBASE: 118 inches

WIDTH: 74 inches
OVERALL LENGTH: 207 inches
WEIGHT: 3,800 pounds

PRICE: N/A

1968 MERCURY COUGAR COUPE	1960 MESKOWSKI RACE CAR	1935 MILLER-FORD RACE CAR	1950 NASH RAMBLER CONVERTIBLE

PAGE: 208	PAGE: 209	PAGES: 210–211	PAGES: 212–213
MAKER Ford Motor Company, Dearborn, Michigan	**MAKER** Wally Meskowski, Indianapolis, Indiana	**MAKER** Miller-Tucker, Detroit, Michigan	**MAKER** Nash-Kelvinator Corporation, Kenosha, Wisconsin
ENGINE V-8, overhead valves, 390 cubic inches	**ENGINE** Meyer and Drake "Offenhauser" inline-4, double overhead cams, 255 cubic inches	**ENGINE** Ford V-8, L-head valves, 221 cubic inches	**ENGINE** Inline-6, L-head valves, 173 cubic inches
TRANSMISSION 3-speed automatic	**TRANSMISSION** 2-speed manual	**TRANSMISSION** 2-speed manual	**TRANSMISSION** 3-speed manual

HORSEPOWER: 335 @ 4,800 rpm
HEIGHT: 52 inches
WHEELBASE: 111 inches

WIDTH: 71 inches
OVERALL LENGTH: 190.5 inches
WEIGHT: 3,134 pounds

PRICE: $3,232

HORSEPOWER: 400 @ 6,000 rpm
HEIGHT: 51 inches
WHEELBASE: 96 inches

WIDTH: 60 inches
OVERALL LENGTH: 161 inches
WEIGHT: 1,895 pounds

COMPETITION HISTORY:
Winner of 13 100-mile championship races, 1960–63, all driven by A. J. Foyt. Won at DuQuoin, Illinois (three times); Langhorne, Pennsylvania (three times); Indiana State Fairgrounds, Indianapolis (twice); Sacramento, California (twice); Trenton, New Jersey (twice); and Phoenix, Arizona.

HORSEPOWER: 150
HEIGHT: 41 inches
WHEELBASE: 100 inches

WIDTH: 68 inches
OVERALL LENGTH: 154.5 inches
WEIGHT: 1,980 pounds

COMPETITION HISTORY:
None. This car did not qualify for the Indianapolis 500.

HORSEPOWER: 82 @ 3,800 rpm
HEIGHT: 59.5 inches
WHEELBASE: 100 inches

WIDTH: 73.5 inches
OVERALL LENGTH: 176 inches
WEIGHT: 2,430 pounds

PRICE: $1,808

1903 OLDSMOBILE CURVED DASH RUNABOUT	1918 OVERLAND MODEL 90 B TOURING CAR	1903 PACKARD MODEL F RUNABOUT	1904 PACKARD MODEL L TOURING CAR

PAGES: 214–215	PAGES: 216–217	PAGES: 218–221	PAGES: 222–223

MAKER
Olds Motor Works, Detroit and Lansing, Michigan

ENGINE
1-cylinder, L-head valves, 95 cubic inches

TRANSMISSION
2-speed manual

MAKER
Willys-Overland Company, Toledo, Ohio

ENGINE
Inline-4, L-head valves, 179 cubic inches

TRANSMISSION
3-speed manual

MAKER
Packard Motor Car Company, Warren, Ohio

ENGINE
Horizontal-1, 184 cubic inches

TRANSMISSION
3-speed manual

MAKER
Packard Motor Car Company, Detroit, Michigan

ENGINE
Inline-4, L-head valves, 242 cubic inches

TRANSMISSION
3-speed manual

HORSEPOWER: 4.5 @ 600 rpm
HEIGHT: 56 inches
WHEELBASE: 66 inches

WIDTH: 62 inches
OVERALL LENGTH: 97 inches
WEIGHT: 650 pounds

PRICE: $650

HORSEPOWER: 32
HEIGHT: 77.5 inches
WHEELBASE: 106 inches

WIDTH: 65 inches
OVERALL LENGTH: 150 inches
WEIGHT: 2,350 pounds

PRICE: $795

HORSEPOWER: 12 @ 850 rpm
HEIGHT: 64.5 inches
WHEELBASE: 88 inches

WIDTH: 69.5 inches
OVERALL LENGTH: 123.5 inches
WEIGHT: 2,200 pounds

PRICE: $2,500

HORSEPOWER: 22 @ 900 rpm
HEIGHT: 94 inches
WHEELBASE: 94 inches

WIDTH: 74 inches
OVERALL LENGTH: 147 inches
WEIGHT: 1,900 pounds

PRICE: $3,000

1950 PLYMOUTH DELUXE SUBURBAN STATION WAGON

PAGES: 224–225

1984 PLYMOUTH VOYAGER MINIVAN

PAGES: 226–227

1965 PONTIAC TEMPEST LeMANS GTO HARDTOP

PAGES: 228–229

1912 RAMBLER KNICKERBOCKER LIMOUSINE

PAGES: 230–231

MAKER
Chrysler Corporation, Highland Park, Michigan

ENGINE
Inline-6, L-head valves, 218 cubic inches

TRANSMISSION
3-speed manual

HORSEPOWER: 97 @ 3,600 rpm
HEIGHT: 71 inches
WHEELBASE: 111 inches

WIDTH: 65.5 inches
OVERALL LENGTH: 186.5 inches
WEIGHT: 3,155 pounds

PRICE: $1,946

MAKER
Chrysler Corporation, Highland Park, Michigan

ENGINE
Inline-4, overhead cam, 135 cubic inches

TRANSMISSION
3-speed automatic

HORSEPOWER: 101 @ 5,600 rpm
HEIGHT: 64 inches
WHEELBASE: 112 inches

WIDTH: 69 inches
OVERALL LENGTH: 176 inches
WEIGHT: 2,911 pounds

PRICE: $12,309

MAKER
General Motors Corporation, Detroit, Michigan

ENGINE
V-8, overhead valves, 389 cubic inches

TRANSMISSION
4-speed manual

HORSEPOWER: 360 @ 5,200 rpm
HEIGHT: 54 inches
WHEELBASE: 115 inches

WIDTH: 73 inches
OVERALL LENGTH: 206 inches
WEIGHT: 3,478 pounds

PRICE: $2,855

MAKER
Thomas B. Jeffery Company, Kenosha, Wisconsin

ENGINE
Inline-4, L-head valves, 432 cubic inches

TRANSMISSION
3-speed manual

HORSEPOWER: 50
HEIGHT: 91.5 inches
WHEELBASE: 128 inches

WIDTH: 67 inches
OVERALL LENGTH: 176 inches
WEIGHT: 4,000 pounds

PRICE: $4,200

1896 RIKER ELECTRIC TRICYCLE

1865 ROPER STEAM CARRIAGE

1913 SCRIPPS-BOOTH ROCKET CYCLECAR PROTOTYPE

1908 STEVENS-DURYEA MODEL U LIMOUSINE

PAGES: 232–233

PAGES: 234–235

PAGES: 236–237

PAGES: 238–239

MAKER
Andrew Lawrence Riker,
Brooklyn, New York

MOTOR
DC

BATTERIES
Lead-acid, 40 volts, 20 cells

MAKER
Sylvester Roper, Roxbury,
Massachusetts

ENGINE
2-cylinder steam, double acting,
3.75-inch bore x 10-inch stroke

MAKER
Scripps-Booth Cyclecar Company,
Detroit, Michigan

ENGINE
V-2, air-cooled, 35 cubic inches

TRANSMISSION
2-speed manual

MAKER
Stevens-Duryea Company,
Chicopee Falls, Massachusetts

ENGINE
Inline-6, L-head valves

TRANSMISSION
3-speed manual

HORSEPOWER: 1
HEIGHT: 44 inches
WHEELBASE: 48 inches

WIDTH: 44.5 inches
OVERALL LENGTH: 81.5 inches
WEIGHT: 488 pounds

PRICE: N/A

HORSEPOWER: Unknown
HEIGHT: 58 inches
WHEELBASE: 54.5 inches

WIDTH: 63 inches
OVERALL LENGTH: 100 inches
WEIGHT: 690 pounds

PRICE: N/A

HORSEPOWER: 10
HEIGHT: 43 inches
WHEELBASE: 100 inches

WIDTH: 41 inches
OVERALL LENGTH: 131 inches
WEIGHT: 670 pounds

PRICE: $385

HORSEPOWER: 35
HEIGHT: 89 inches
WHEELBASE: 114 inches

WIDTH: 65.5 inches
OVERALL LENGTH: 163 inches
WEIGHT: 3,400 pounds

PRICE: $4,500

1951 STUDEBAKER CHAMPION STARLIGHT COUPE

1965 GOLDENROD LAND SPEED RACE CAR

1906 THOMAS FLYER TOURING CAR

1966 TOYOTA CORONA SEDAN

PAGES: 240–243

PAGES: 244–247

PAGES: 248–251

PAGE: 252

MAKER
Studebaker Corporation, South Bend, Indiana

ENGINE
Inline-6, L-head valves, 170 cubic inches

TRANSMISSION
3-speed automatic

HORSEPOWER: 85 @ 4,000 rpm
HEIGHT: 60.5 inches
WHEELBASE: 115 inches

WIDTH: 70.5 inches
OVERALL LENGTH: 197.5 inches
WEIGHT: 2,675 pounds

PRICE: $1,985

MAKER
Bob and Bill Summers, Riverside, California

ENGINE
Four Chrysler V-8s, hemispherical combustion chambers, overhead valves, 426 cubic inches each

TRANSMISSION
Two Spicer 5-speed manuals with first gear removed, simultaneous shifting via special Hurst shifter

HORSEPOWER: 2,400 @ 6,700 rpm
HEIGHT: 42 inches to top of tail fin, 28 inches to top of engine hood
WHEELBASE: 207 inches

WIDTH: 48 inches
OVERALL LENGTH: 384 inches
WEIGHT: 8,000 pounds

COMPETITION HISTORY:
Set the record for wheel-driven vehicles at 409.277 mph at Bonneville Salt Flats in Utah. The record stood for 26 years. Driver: Bob Summers.

MAKER
E. R. Thomas Motor Company, Buffalo, New York

ENGINE
Inline-4, T-head valves, 523 cubic inches

TRANSMISSION
4-speed manual

HORSEPOWER: 50
HEIGHT: 99 inches (with top)
WHEELBASE: 118 inches

WIDTH: 69 inches
OVERALL LENGTH: 168 inches
WEIGHT: 3,200 pounds

PRICE: $3,500

MAKER
Toyota Motor Corporation, Tokyo, Japan

ENGINE
Inline-4, overhead valves, 116 cubic inches

TRANSMISSION
3-speed automatic

HORSEPOWER: 90 @ 4,600 rpm
HEIGHT: 56 inches
WHEELBASE: 95.5 inches

WIDTH: 61 inches
OVERALL LENGTH: 162 inches
WEIGHT: 2,100 pounds

PRICE: $1,745

2002 TOYOTA PRIUS SEDAN	1948 TUCKER 48 SEDAN	1949 VOLKSWAGEN SEDAN	1959 VOLKSWAGEN WESTFALIA CAMPER

PAGE: 253	PAGES: 254–257	PAGES: 258–259	PAGES: 260–261

MAKER Toyota Motor Corporation, Tokyo, Japan	**MAKER** Tucker Corporation, Chicago, Illinois	**MAKER** Volkswagenwerk GmbH, Wolfsburg, West Germany	**MAKER/CAMPING EQUIPMENT** Volkswagen GmbH, Wolfsburg, West Germany/Westfalia-Werke, Wiedenbrueck, West Germany
ENGINE/MOTOR/ BATTERIES Inline-4, double overhead cam, 91 cubic inches/DC, permanent magnet/38 nickel-metal hydride, 273 volts	**ENGINE** Horizontally opposed 6, overhead valves, 334 cubic inches	**ENGINE** Horizontally opposed 4, overhead valves, 69 cubic inches	**ENGINE** Horizontally opposed 4, 73 cubic inches
TRANSMISSION Continuously variable automatic	**TRANSMISSION** 4-speed manual	**TRANSMISSION** 4-speed manual	**TRANSMISSION** 4-speed manual

HORSEPOWER: Gasoline, 76 @ 5,000 rpm / Electric, 55 @ 5,600 rpm HEIGHT: 57.5 inches WHEELBASE: 100.5 inches WIDTH: 66.5 inches OVERALL LENGTH: 169.5 inches WEIGHT: 2,765 pounds PRICE: $19,995	HORSEPOWER: 116 @ 3,200 rpm HEIGHT: 80 inches WHEELBASE: 130 inches WIDTH: 64.5 inches OVERALL LENGTH: 219 inches WEIGHT: 4,235 pounds PRICE: $2,450	HORSEPOWER: 30 @ 3,300 rpm HEIGHT: 61 inches WHEELBASE: 94.5 inches WIDTH: 60.5 inches OVERALL LENGTH: 160 inches WEIGHT: 1,600 pounds PRICE: $1,280	HORSEPOWER: 36 @ 3,700 rpm HEIGHT: 76.5 inches WHEELBASE: 94.5 inches WIDTH: 69 inches OVERALL LENGTH: 166 inches WEIGHT: 2,569 pounds PRICE: $2,737

1907 WHITE MODEL G STEAM TOURING CAR

PAGES: 262–265

MAKER
White Company, Cleveland, Ohio

ENGINE
2-cylinder compound steam, HP cylinder 3 inches bore x 4.5 inches stroke, LP cylinder 6 inches bore x 4.5 inches stroke, 159 cubic inches

HORSEPOWER: 30
HEIGHT: 74 inches
WHEELBASE: 115 inches

WIDTH: 66 inches
OVERALL LENGTH: 189 inches
WEIGHT: 3,635 pounds

PRICE: $3,500

1933 WILLYS DRAG RACER

PAGES: 266–267

MAKER
George Montgomery, Dayton, Ohio

ENGINE
Ford V-8, single overhead cam, supercharged, 427 cubic inches

TRANSMISSION
3-speed automatic

HORSEPOWER: 1,200
HEIGHT: 65 inches
WHEELBASE: 100 inches

WIDTH: 72 inches
OVERALL LENGTH: 161 inches
WEIGHT: 2,245 pounds

COMPETITION HISTORY:
Winner of National Hot Rod Association U.S. Nationals class championships in 1959, 1960, 1961, 1963, 1964, and 1966 and Winternational class championship in 1967. Winner of Little Eliminator at 1959 and 1960 U.S. Nationals and Middle Eliminator at 1963 U.S. Nationals.

1943 WILLYS-OVERLAND JEEP RUNABOUT

PAGES: 268–269

MAKER
Willys-Overland Company, Toledo, Ohio

ENGINE
Inline-4, L-head valves, 134 cubic inches

TRANSMISSION
3-speed manual

HORSEPOWER: 54 @ 4,000 rpm
HEIGHT: 72 inches
WHEELBASE: 80 inches

WIDTH: 62 inches
OVERALL LENGTH: 132 inches
WEIGHT: 2,450 pounds

PRICE: $1,447

1916 WOODS DUAL-POWER HYBRID COUPE

PAGES: 270–271

MAKER
Woods Motor Vehicle Company, Chicago, Illinois

ENGINE
Inline-4, L-head valves, 69 cubic inches

MOTOR
DC, lead-acid batteries, 48 volts, 24 cells

HORSEPOWER: Gasoline, 14 / Electric, unknown
HEIGHT: 82.5 inches
WHEELBASE: 110 inches

WIDTH: 63 inches
OVERALL LENGTH: 160 inches
WEIGHT: 3,000 pounds

PRICE: $2,650

LIST OF MOTOR VEHICLES IN THE HENRY FORD COLLECTION *

The one hundred vehicles featured in this book are on display to the public. This list represents the entire collection, including those vehicles not displayed. The accession numbers are unique museum identification numbers. Bringing an object into a museum and documenting and storing it is called "accessioning."

PASSENGER CARS

MAKE	MODEL AND BODY STYLE	YEAR	ACCESSION NUMBER
Alcoa	Aluminum Sedan	1925	33.102.1
American Austin	Model A Roadster	1930	64.76.1
Apperson	Jack Rabbit Touring Car	1916	58.21.1
Auburn	Convertible Sedan	1930	78.88.1
Auto Red Bug	Buckboard Runabout (used by Edsel Ford's children)	1928	48.17.3
Autocar	Type V Runabout	1898	54.31.1
Baker	Runabout	1901	35.213.1
Baker	Victoria (used by First Ladies Ellen Wilson and Edith Wilson)	1912	28.264.1
Benz	Velocipede	1893	30.1740.5
Benz	Comfortable Runabout	1897	30.1725.1
Benz	Parsifal Touring Car	1903	30.1725.3
Brewster	Knight Town Landaulet	1915	41.40.1
Brush	Model E24 Runabout	1911	29.2123.1
Budd	XT-Bird Convertible	1961	97.32.2
Budd	XR-400 Convertible	1962	97.32.1
Bugatti	Royale Type 41 Convertible	1931	58.86.1
Buick	Model F Touring Car	1908	32.730.1
Buick	Model 10 Tonneau	1909	87.65.1
Buick	Model 72R Roadmaster Sedan	1950	86.176.1
Buick	Riviera Coupe	1963	87.69.1
Cadillac	Model A Runabout	1903	29.509.1
Cadillac	Type 51 Touring Car	1915	00.3.2427
Cadillac	Sixty Special Sedan	1938	89.386.1
Cadillac	Eldorado Biarritz Convertible	1959	86.48.1
Chalmers-Detroit	Model E Roadster	1909	00.119.2
Chevrolet	Series H Royal Mail Roadster	1915	58.77.1
Chevrolet	"Copper Cooled" Series C Coupe (air-cooled engine)	1923	00.136.125
Chevrolet	International Model AC Sedan	1929	61.16.1
Chevrolet	Bel Air Hardtop	1955	86.113.1
Chevrolet	Corvette Roadster	1955	72.108.1
Chevrolet	Bel Air Convertible	1956	83.94.1
Chevrolet	Corvair Sedan	1960	85.64.1
Chrysler	Model B-70 Touring Car	1924	93.96.1
Chrysler	Series 80 Imperial Sportif Convertible	1927	62.9.1
Chrysler	Custom Imperial Landau Sedan (personal car of Walter P. Chrysler)	1932	60.35.1
Chrysler	Crown Imperial Parade Phaeton	1940	60.35.2
Chrysler	New Yorker Sedan	1950	87.193.1
Chrysler	Turbine Sedan	1956	66.52.1
Chrysler	Newport Sedan	1973	2011.329.1
Columbia	Mark V Victoria	1901	31.282.1
Comuta-Car	Runabout	1980	2006.84.1
Continental	Mark II Sedan	1956	73.34.1
Cord	812 Convertible	1937	57.25.1
Cornell-Liberty	Safety Car Sedan	1957	92.172.1
Cornell-Liberty	Safety Car Sedan	1961	92.172.2
Crosley	Hotshot Roadster	1951	77.43.1

PASSENGER CARS

MAKE	MODEL AND BODY STYLE	YEAR	ACCESSION NUMBER
Crowder College	"Phoenix" Solar-Powered Car	1984	88.330.1
Daimler	Victoria Town Cabriolet	1897	30.304.3
De Dion-Bouton	Motorette Runabout	1900	31.94.1
De Soto	Airflow Series SE Sedan	1934	86.52.1
De Soto	Fireflite Hardtop	1957	93.151.1
Detroit Electric	Model 47 Brougham	1914	38.372.2
Detroit Electric	Model 90 Coupe	1922	34.371.1
Doble	Phaeton #9 Touring Car	1924	36.520.27
Dodge	Omni Sedan	1978	2011.329.2
Dodge	Ram Quad Cab Pickup Truck	1998	2011.124.1
Dodge Brothers	Model 30 Touring Car	1918	64.134.1
Duesenberg	Model J Convertible Victoria	1931	62.9.2
Duryea	Runabout	1896	72.127.1
Duryea	Trap	1899	36.110.1
Edison	Runabout (built under the direction of Thomas A. Edison)	1889	29.1337.1
Edison2	Sedan	2010	2012.32.1
Edsel	Citation Hardtop (serial number 1)	1958	58.91.1
Elmore	Model 30 Touring Car	1908	29.176.3
Essex	Coach Sedan	1924	83.120.1
Ford	Quadricycle	1896	00.2.93
Ford	Quadricycle, 1963 Replica	1896	63.159.1
Ford	Quadricycle, 1991 Replica	1896	91.296.1
Ford	Runabout	1898	34.567.1
Ford	Roadster (built by Detroit Automobile Company)	1901	00.136.126
Ford	Runabout (built by Henry Ford Company)	1902	35.397.1
Ford	Model A Runabout	1903	00.136.137
Ford	Model A Tonneau	1903	25.157.1
Ford	Model C Tonneau	1904	00.3.8032
Ford	Model C Tonneau	1904	00.4.3162
Ford	Model B Touring Car	1905	00.136.121
Ford	Model F Phaeton	1905	57.77.2
Ford	Model N Runabout	1906	85.115.1
Ford	Model K Touring	1907	00.3.2425
Ford	Model R Runabout	1907	00.1259.1
Ford	Model S Roadster	1908	29.1009.1
Ford	Model T Touring Car	1909	57.77.1
Ford	Model T Touring Car	1913	57.21.1
Ford	Cyclecar Roadster	1914	00.2.142
Ford	Model T Touring Car	1914	71.82.1
Ford	Model T Touring Car (used in Greenfield Village programs)	1916	2003.86.1
Ford	Model T Touring Car (used in Henry Ford Museum programs)	1917	95.36.1
Ford	Model T Sedan	1919	61.136.1
Ford	Model T Coupe (personal car of Henry Ford)	1919	38.372.1

MAKE	MODEL AND BODY STYLE	YEAR	ACCESSION NUMBER
Ford	Model T Touring Car (used in Greenfield Village programs)	1921	2001.62.1
Ford	Model T Station Wagon (used in Greenfield Village programs)	1923	59.104.1
Ford	Model T Touring Car (used in Greenfield Village programs)	1923	94.41.1
Ford	Model T Touring Car (used in Greenfield Village programs)	1924	2001.73.1
Ford	Model T Touring Car (used in Greenfield Village programs)	1924	96.89.1
Ford	Model T Touring Car (used in Greenfield Village programs)	1926	2002.169.1
Ford	Model T Touring Car (used in Greenfield Village programs)	1927	2002.166.1
Ford	Model T Touring Car (15 millionth Ford and last Model T)	1927	00.136.124
Ford	Model A Touring Car (personal car of Thomas A. Edison, serial number 1)	1928	43.30.1
Ford	Model A Sedan	1928	94.118.1
Ford	Model A Coupe (personal car of Henry Ford)	1929	38.372.3
Ford	Model A Roadster	1929	82.85.1
Ford	Model A Station Wagon	1929	70.61.1
Ford	Model A Sedan	1929	83.10.1
Ford	Model A Touring Car	1930	76.143.1
Ford	Model 18 Victoria	1932	2002.167.1
Ford	Model 18 Cabriolet	1932	65.6.1
Ford	Model 18 Roadster (hot rod)	1932	87.141.1
Ford	Model 48 Touring Sedan	1935	83.162.1
Ford	DeLuxe Convertible Coupe	1939	55.24.1
Ford	V-8 Super Deluxe Fordor Sedan (personal car of Henry Ford)	1942	58.74.1
Ford	V-8 Club Coupe	1949	2003.47.1
Ford	Tudor Sedan (serial number 1)	1949	48.6.1
Ford	Sunliner Convertible (1953 Indianapolis 500 Pace Car)	1953	54.8.1
Ford	X-100 Semi-Convertible	1953	58.73.1
Ford	Thunderbird Convertible	1956	2003.36.1
Ford	Thunderbird Convertible	1956	76.55.1
Ford	Mustang I Roadster	1962	74.57.1
Ford	Mustang Convertible	1965	2003.46.1
Ford	Mustang Convertible (serial number 1)	1965	66.47.1
Ford	Escort GLX Sedan (serial number 1)	1981	80.84.1
Ford	Econocar Coupe	1982	88.427.1
Ford	Taurus LX Sedan	1986	90.201.1
Ford	Explorer Sport Utility Vehicle	1991	2011.392.1
Ford	Adrenalin Pickup Truck	1996	2003.143.4
Ford	Alpe Limited Crossover	1998	2003.143.2
Ford	Focus Sedan	2009	2011.196.1
Ford	Thunderbird Hardtop (serial number 1)	2011	2001.100.1
Franklin	Type E Runabout	1905	60.61.1
Franklin	Airman Sport Sedan (personal car of Charles A. Lindbergh)	1928	40.222.1
General Motors	EV1 Coupe	1997	2002.76.1

MAKE	MODEL AND BODY STYLE	YEAR	ACCESSION NUMBER
Haynes-Apperson	Two-Cylinder Surrey	1901	00.3.5211
Holsman	Highwheeler Runabout	1903	00.241.1
Honda	Accord DX Sedan	1989	2011.197.1
Hudson	Limousine	1951	75.56.1
Hupmobile	Model 20 Coupe	1911	35.95.1
Hupmobile	Series A Coupe	1929	87.24.1
International Harvester	Model G Roadster	1910	29.238.1
Kaiser	Traveler Sedan	1949	82.98.1
LaSalle	Series 303 Roadster	1927	81.142.1
LaSalle	Series 50 Coupe	1937	81.9.1
Lincoln	Model L Touring Car (personal car of Thomas A. Edison)	1923	43.30.2
Lincoln	Model L Convertible	1929	78.5.1
Lincoln	Zephyr Sedan (serial number 1)	1936	38.177.1
Lincoln	Model K Landaulet	1937	73.32.1
Lincoln	Presidential Limousine	1939	50.11.1
Lincoln	Continental Cabriolet	1941	77.92.1
Lincoln	Continental Cabriolet (personal car of Edsel Ford)	1941	56.79.1
Lincoln	Presidential Limousine	1950	67.74.1
Lincoln	Continental Presidential Limousine	1961	78.4.1
Lincoln	Continental Presidential Limousine	1972	92.104.1
Lincoln	Sentinel Sedan	1996	2003.143.1
Lincoln	Blackwood Pickup Truck	1998	2003.143.3
Locomobile	Runabout	1899	86.141.1
Marmon	Model 34 Roadster	1921	78.119.1
Maxwell	Model AB Runabout	1911	30.898.2
Mercer	22-72 Touring Car (used by Edsel Ford)	1916	00.240.1
Mercury	99A Town Sedan (serial number 1)	1939	45.36.1
Mercury	Series 9CM Convertible (customized)	1949	92.110.1
Mercury	Cougar XR-7 Coupe	1968	2002.42.1
Meyers Manx	Dune Buggy	1970	90.120.1
MG	TC Roadster	1947	87.72.1
Nash	Advanced Six Sedan	1926	61.118.3
Nash	Rambler Convertible	1950	87.176.1
Northern	Single Runabout	1904	00.65.103
Oakland	Model 24 Runabout	1911	60.69.1
Oldsmobile	Curved Dash Runabout	1903	30.1303.1
Overland	Model 15 Runabout	1904	60.113.2
Overland	Light Four 90 Touring Car	1917	99.22.1
Overland	Model 90 B Touring Car	1918	87.23.1
Owen Magnetic	Six Touring Car	1915	30.929.1
Packard	Model F Runabout ("Old Pacific")	1903	35.455.2
Packard	Model L Touring Car	1904	71.126.1
Packard	Twin Six Touring Car	1916	35.402.1
Packard	Model 626 Roadster	1929	76.103.1
Packard	Twelve Convertible Victoria	1939	78.65.1
Peerless	Model 29 Brewster Victoria	1911	35.309.1
Pierce Arrow	Two-Cylinder Roadster	1904	00.65.104
Plymouth	Model PD Coupe	1933	84.89.1
Plymouth	Deluxe Suburban Station Wagon	1950	88.217.1
Plymouth	Voyager Minivan	1984	90.248.1
Pontiac	Tempest LeMans GTO Hardtop	1965	87.70.1
Pope-Hartford	Model B Tonneau	1904	29.181.1

PASSENGER CARS

MAKE	MODEL AND BODY STYLE	YEAR	ACCESSION NUMBER
Rambler	Model L Tonneau	1904	36.520.55
Rambler	Knickerbocker Limousine	1912	61.118.1
Riker	Tricycle	1896	30.328.4
Rolls-Royce	Phantom II Limousine	1926	38.472.1
Roper	Steam Carriage	1865	30.966.1
Saxon	Model 14 Roadster	1916	36.520.46
Scripps-Booth	Rocket Cyclecar	1913	41.300.1
Sears	Model H Motor Buggy	1909	64.19.1
Selden	Motor Buggy	1907	63.22.1
Stanley Steamer	Model 60 Runabout	1910	35.495.1
Star	Model C Station Wagon	1923	83.16.1
Stevens-Duryea	Model U Limousine	1908	25.88.1
Stoddard-Dayton	Special Touring Car	1912	00.3.2428
Studebaker	Champion Starlight Coupe	1951	85.80.1
Studebaker	Avanti Coupe	1963	76.49.1
Stutz	Bearcat Roadster	1923	67.19.1
Thomas	Flyer Touring Car	1906	68.111.1
Toyota	Corona Sedan	1966	87.120.1
Toyota	Prius Sedan	2002	2006.74.1
Tucker	48 Sedan	1948	58.62.1
Univ. of Michigan	"Sunrunner" Solar-Powered Car	1990	91.6.1
Volkswagen	Type 1 Sedan	1949	82.47.1
Volkswagen	Type 2 Westfalia Camper	1959	87.153.1
Warrior	Touring Car	1974	2001.162.1
Welch	Model G Touring Car	1907	29.358.1
White	Model G Steam Touring Car	1907	36.520.3
Wills Sainte Claire	Model W-6 Roadster	1926	46.5.1
Willys-Knight	Model 67 Touring Car	1924	83.120.3
Willys-Overland	Jeep Runabout	1943	87.154.1
Winton	Touring Car	1900	37.220.1
Woods	Dual-Power Coupe	1916	28.436.1
Woods Mobilette	Model 5A Roadster	1917	36.321.1

RACE CARS

MAKE	TYPE OF RACING	YEAR	ACCESSION NUMBER
Beatty Lakester	Land Speed	1951	2009.140.1
Buck & Thompson Dragster	Drag	1960	89.327.1
Chrysler 300-B	Stock Car	1956	2003.13.1
Ford Sweepstakes	Dirt Track	1901	00.136.123
Ford Sweepstakes, 2001 Replica	Dirt Track	1901	2008.132.1
Ford 999	Dirt Track	1902	19.3.1
Ford 999, 1965 Replica	Dirt Track	1902	65.111.1
Ford 666	Dirt Track	1907	00.3.4722
Ford Model T Special	Dirt Track, Hill Climb	1910	00.136.128
Ford Mark IV	Sports Car	1967	71.83.1
Ford Thunderbird	Stock Car	1987	88.84.1
Locomobile Old 16	Vanderbilt Cup	1906	97.9.1.1
Lotus-Ford 38	Indy Car	1965	77.21.1
March-Cosworth 84C	Indy Car	1984	85.24.1

RACE CARS

MAKE	TYPE OF RACING	YEAR	ACCESSION NUMBER
McLaren–Offenhauser M16B	Indy Car	1972	2006.24.1
Meskowski	Dirt Track	1960	2008.101.1
Miller-Ford	Indy Car	1935	69.137.1
Riker Electric Torpedo	Land Speed	1901	30.328.2
Summers Brothers Goldenrod	Land Speed	1965	2002.103.1
Willys Gasser	Drag	1933	2003.20.1

COMMERCIAL VEHICLES

MAKE	MODEL AND BODY STYLE	YEAR	ACCESSION NUMBER
Bluebird	School Bus	1927	2007.73.1
Checker	Marathon Taxicab	1981	90.370.1
Dodge	Airflow Tank Truck	1939	84.159.1
Federal	Stake Truck	1910	59.106.1
Federal	45M Truck Tractor	1952	88.381.1
FMC	2900R Motorhome	1972	95.23.1
Ford	Model T Taxicab	1917	83.120.2
Ford	Model TT Stake Truck	1925	78.74.1
Ford	Model AA Truck	1930	65.107.1
Ford	Econoline Van	1965	89.288.1
Ford	C-700 Truck	1974	90.191.1
Ford	Ranger FX4 Truck	1992	2002.62.1
Ford-Smith	Model T Form-A-Truck	1911	52.3.1
GMC	Model 16 Express Pickup Truck	1918	72.71.1
GMC	TDH-3610 Transit Bus (Rosa Parks Bus)	1948	2001.154.1
Graham Brothers	Nomad Motor Home	1928	81.97.1
International Harvester	Model A Truck	1911	36.520.12
International Harvester	Model AW Truck	1912	36.520.14
Lincoln	Refrigerated Vehicle	1922	28.743.1
Nash	Quad Truck	1918	00.3.13569
Oscar Mayer	Weinermobile	1952	91.143.1
Packard	Twin Six Camp Truck	1916	37.115.1
Rapid	Bus	1906	68.112.1
White	Camping Truck	1921	00.2.56
Wood	Electric Delivery Truck	1900	32.570.1
Yellow Cab	Taxicab	1925	88.333.1

VEHICLES ON LOAN TO THE HENRY FORD

MAKE	MODEL	YEAR
Ford	F-100 Pickup Truck	1956
Ford/Wood Bros	Fusion Stock Car	2011
Honda	Accord LX Sedan	1983
Moore/Unser	Pikes Peak Hill Climb Racing Car	1958

Exposing History

By Mark Harmer

Photographer

For as long as I can remember, I've had a passion for planes, trains, and automobiles. I started with Matchbox and Hot Wheels cars and moved on to minibikes and motorcycles. My first car was a British Racing Green MGB Roadster. During college, I was fortunate to intern under Dick James, one of the world's foremost automotive photographers. After graduation, I worked as a photographer for the Ford Motor Company for four years before setting out on my own.

I have had the opportunity to do advertising photography for some of the best automotive manufacturers in the world, shooting cars all over the country. But in February 2011, with the help of my assistants Larry Lambrecht and Andrew Trahan, I started photographing The Henry Ford Collection of automobiles.

We set up a full-blown automotive photography studio, laying out a paintable floor on top of the famous parquet floor of Henry Ford Museum. We assembled our thirty-two-foot light box, which was supported on each corner by a small crane. All the windows in our corner of the museum were covered to control the light. In addition, we used small lights to create highlights and shadows in order to best display each vehicle's shape and texture.

The presidential limos and the large trucks had to be photographed in position, since they could not be moved to our corner studio. We suspended our light box on scaffolding, and after the museum closed, we slowly rolled it through the halls to place it over each photographic subject. Transporting the light box was like maneuvering a dirigible through the museum—quite a sight!

The museum staff opened doors, hoods, and trunks to give our cameras access to the cars inside and out. Some parts of the cars had not been seen by the public in twenty years. I'll never forget looking through the open door of the Kennedy limousine late at night and thinking of the events surrounding this car and how they changed history. And as a racing fan, I was in awe when the Jim Clark Indy-winning Lotus was rolled onto the set. This car changed the face of racing in one afternoon and brought on the demise of the front engine roadster.

One of the first questions I would ask as the next vehicle was rolled onto the set was, "Can we see what's under the hood?" My favorite engine was the 1906 Locomobile "Old 16." The incredible motor of this car displaces 990 cubic inches with four cylinders and is made of cast iron, brass, copper, aluminum, steel, and wood.

Of course, the job couldn't have been completed without the help of the incredible team at The Henry Ford. Many hours of preparation were spent on each automobile before it could be photographed, including cars that had been in storage for years. Photographing this collection was the opportunity of a lifetime. I will forever be proud of the work we accomplished in a back corner of The Henry Ford.

Mark Harmer

The Henry Ford in Dearborn, Michigan, is the world's premier history destination and a national historic landmark that celebrates American history and innovation. With an unparalleled collection of authentic artifacts that changed the world and the stories of some of the greatest innovators that ever lived, The Henry Ford is a significant educational resource for understanding America's history of innovation, ingenuity, and resourcefulness. Its mission is to use its unparalleled assets to inspire future generations to help create a better future.

The institution holds twenty-six million authentic artifacts and documents, including Thomas Edison's Menlo Park laboratory, the bus on which Rosa Parks refused to give up her seat, the Wright Brothers' home and cycle shop, and Buckminster Fuller's Dymaxion House. Five distinct attractions captivate and inspire more than 1.5 million visitors annually: Henry Ford Museum, Greenfield Village, The Ford Rouge Factory Tour, The Benson Ford Research Center, and The Henry Ford IMAX Theatre. The Henry Ford is also home to Henry Ford Academy, a five-hundred-student public charter high school founded in partnership with The Henry Ford, Ford Motor Company, and Wayne County Public Schools.

The Henry Ford provides a unique cultural environment, both educational and inspirational, designed to effect positive change in the world by fueling the spirit of American innovation and inspiring a "can-do" entrepreneurial mindset and culture.

Mission
The Henry Ford provides unique educational experiences based on authentic objects, stories, and lives from America's traditions of ingenuity, resourcefulness and innovation. Our purpose is to inspire people to learn from these traditions to help shape a better future.

The Henry Ford
20900 Oakwood Boulevard
Dearborn, Michigan 48124-5029
313-982-6001
TheHenryFord.org

Driving America: The Henry Ford Automotive Collection was developed by Beckon Books. Beckon develops and publishes custom books for leading cultural attractions, corporations, and nonprofit organizations. Beckon Books is an imprint of Southwestern Publishing Group, Inc., 2451 Atrium Way, Nashville, TN 37214. Southwestern Publishing Group, Inc., is a wholly owned subsidiary of Southwestern, Inc., Nashville, Tennessee.

Christopher G. Capen, *President, Beckon Books*
Monika Stout, *Design/Production*
Betsy Holt, *Editor*
www.beckonbooks.com
877-311-0155

Library of Congress Control Number: 2013937276
Deluxe Edition ISBN: 978-1-935442-26-4
Collectors Edition ISBN: 978-1-935442-29-5

Printed in China
10 9 8 7 6 5 4 3 2 1